Meeting the Needs

of Your Most Able Pupils:

ART

Other titles in the series

Meeting the Needs of Your Most Able Pupils: Design and Technology
Louise T. Davies
1 84312 330 4

Meeting the Needs of Your Most Able Pupils: Music
Jonathan Savage
1 84312 347 9

Meeting the Needs of Your Most Able Pupils: Physical Education and Sport
David Morley and Richard Bailey
1 84312 334 7

Meeting the Needs
of Your Most Able Pupils:
ART

Kim Earle

David Fulton Publishers

David Fulton Publishers Ltd
The Chiswick Centre, 414 Chiswick High Road, London W4 5TF

www.fultonpublishers.co.uk
www.onestopeducation.co.uk

David Fulton Publishers is a division of Granada Learning Limited, part of ITV plc.

Note: the right of Kim Earle to be identified as the author of this work has been asserted by her in accordance with the Copyright, Designs and Patents Act 1988.

British Library Cataloguing in Publication data
A catalogue record for this book is available from the British Library.

ISBN: 1 84312 331 2

10 9 8 7 6 5 4 3 2 1

Series production editor: Andrew Welsh
Typeset by Servis Filmsetting Ltd, Manchester
Printed and bound in Great Britain

This book is dedicated to my husband Chad,
my daughter Ariki, my son Joe and my mum Rose.
Their support and encouragement is much appreciated.

Thank you!

Contents

Colour plates

Working with artists-in-residence:

Work produced by students and a digital artist-in-residence for the 'Chartres' project discussed in Chapter 6

Year 7 clay portraits produced during artist residency

Project for able pupils in Year 10 working with a fine artist

Able pupils working outside the classroom as extension and enrichment:

Masterclass at Liverpool John Moores University

Museum visits and workshops

Examples of work by able pupils in Years 9, 10 and 11:

Textile pieces based on Pop Art and Identity

Research on African and Indian art and artefacts

Examples of large-scale card sculptures

Textile work

Foreword

It is inconceivable that a school can claim to be taking forward the personalisation agenda seriously without having a robust approach to gifted and talented education.

(Rt Hon. Jacqui Smith MP, Minister of State, Schools and
14–19 Learners, January 2006)

Effective schools provide an appropriate education for all pupils. They focus on the needs of individuals and design their offer to take account of the needs of the main recognised groups. Gifted and talented pupils are now a recognised group within each school. For a school to be effective it must plan its provision for these pupils, identify those who will benefit and monitor the effectiveness of their offer through its impact on the learning outcomes of pupils. This formalises the position of gifted and talented education and ensures that the needs of the most able are not overlooked.

Since 2000 we have begun to see the impact of a clear focus on the needs of gifted and talented pupils in the education system. The Qualifications and Curriculum Authority (QCA) and the National Strategies have begun to focus on this group and to provide materials and training to support teachers. The Office for Standards in Education (Ofsted) takes their needs into account when assessing the performance of a school and the government has established the National Academy for Gifted and Talented Youth (NAGTY) to steer this agenda.

NAGTY's role is to drive forward improvements in gifted and talented education by developing a national, government-supported catalyst that can provide leadership and support for professionals working in this field. To achieve this, it works with students, parents, teachers, education professionals, specialist providers, universities and business. Children and young people are at the heart of the Academy's mission. NAGTY aims to ensure that all children and young people, regardless of background, have access to the formal and informal learning opportunities they need to help them convert their potential into high achievement.

Gifted education in England is very much part of the overall education system and deeply embedded in it. The English model of gifted and talented education is a description of this approach and the rationale for it. Provision is rooted in day-to-day classroom provision and enhanced by additional, more advanced opportunities offered both within school and outside of it. Giftedness is a term used to describe children or adults who have the *capacity* to achieve high levels of expertise or performance. Giftedness in childhood could be described as 'expertise in its development phase'. Therefore, the education of gifted and talented pupils should focus on expertise development. Giftedness is developmental and is developed through individuals gaining access to appropriate opportunities and support. Performance levels are directly affected by availability of appropriate opportunities and support. Direct intervention with individuals can help reverse the effect of socioeconomic disadvantage or other lack of support.

Provision for gifted children should be made in ordinary schools as part of the day-to-day educational offer. This core provision should be supplemented by access to enhanced opportunities offered both within and beyond the school. Schools should themselves be diverse and distinctive in nature and so offer specific opportunities to develop certain aptitudes and parents should be seen as co-educators with a key role in supporting learning.

This series of books is a welcome addition to the literature base. It aims to help teachers make the English model a reality. In this model every teacher needs to be a teacher of the gifted. They need to understand how to teach the gifted and talented and have both the confidence and the skills to make that a reality on a day-to-day basis. While there are generic aspects to provision for gifted and talented pupils, the majority of classroom provision is subject-based and so it is through a subject approach that most teachers will consider the needs of their most able pupils. This series of books aims to help teachers within the subject domains to become more effective teachers of the gifted and talented pupils in their class. It builds on the emerging frameworks supplied by DfES, NAGTY and the government agencies and interprets them within a subject-specific context.

Without doubt this series of books will be a considerable help to both individual teachers and to schools seeking to improve provision for their gifted and talented children and young people.

PROFESSOR DEBORAH EYRE
Director, NAGTY

Acknowledgements

I would like to thank the following people, schools and organisations that have helped contribute to the compilation of this book in so many ways. Without their support this book could not have been compiled. A huge 'thank you' to: St Helens Council; Margaret Buckley, Eileen Horrocks, Kevin Kelly, Sue Buckley, Sheena Smith, Fred Leather, Dorrie Halliday, Peter Oakley, Martin Maris, Gill Curry; St Aelred's Catholic Technology College, St Augustine's RC High School (Visual Arts), De La Salle School Performing Arts, Haydock High School, Sutton Manor Primary School, BBC Philharmonic, University of the Arts London, and above all the pupils of St Helens who graciously allowed their artwork to be used in this book!

Contributors to the series

The author

Kim Earle is a former secondary head of art and design and is currently an able pupils and arts consultant for St Helens. She has been a member of DfES steering groups, is an Artsmark validator, a subject editor for G&TWISE and is a practising designer jeweller and enameller.

Series editor

Gwen Goodhew's many and varied roles within the field of gifted and talented education have included school G&T coordinator, director of Wirral Able Children Centre, Knowsley Excellence in Cities (EiC) G&T coordinator, member of the DfES G&T Advisory Group, teacher trainer and consultant. She has written and edited numerous reports and articles on the subject and co-authored *Providing for Able Children* with Linda Evans.

Other authors

Design and Technology

During the writing of the D&T book **Louise T. Davies** was a part-time subject adviser for design and technology at the QCA (Qualifications and Curriculum Authority), and part of the KS3 National Strategy team for the D&T programme. She has authored over 40 D&T books and award-winning multimedia resources. She is currently deputy chief executive of the Design and Technology Association.

Music

Jonathan Savage is a senior lecturer in music education at the Institute of Education, Manchester Metropolitan University. Until 2001 he was head of music at Debenham High School, an 11–16 comprehensive school in Suffolk. He is a co-author of a new resource introducing computer game sound design to the Key Stage 3 curriculum (www.sound2game.net) and managing director of UCan.tv (www.ucan.tv), a company specialising in the production of educational software and hardware. When not doing all of this, he is busy parenting four very musically talented children!

Physical Education and Sport

David Morley has taught physical education in a number of secondary schools. He is currently senior lecturer in physical education at Leeds Metropolitan University and the director of the national DfES-funded 'Development in PE' project which is part of the Gifted and Talented strand of the PE, School Sport and Club Links (PESSCL) project. He is also a member of the team responsible for developing resources for national Multi-skill Clubs and is the founder and director of the Carnegie Regional Multi-skill Camp held at Leeds Met Carnegie.

Richard Bailey is a professor of pedagogy at Roehampton University, having previously worked at Reading and Leeds Metropolitan University, and at Canterbury Christ Church University where he was director of the Centre for Physical Education Research. He is a well-known author and speaker on physical education, sport and education.

Contents of the CD

The CD accompanying this book may be used by the purchasing individual/ organisation only. It contains files which may be amended to suit particular situations, or individual learning needs, and printed out for use by the purchaser.

Policy and management

1. Ofsted – Expectations of schools in relation to able pupils (Appendix 1.1)
2. Departmental procedure (Appendix 2.1)
3. Audit guidelines
4. Internal audit (Appendix 2.2)
5. Audit of current provision
6. Evaluation tools
7. Planning future provision
8. Departmental action plan (Appendix 2.3)
9. INSET – What do we mean by able in art and design
10. INSET – Enrichment opportunities for developing talent in art
11. INSET – Updating units of work in art extension activities
12. More able pupil nomination sheet
13. Sample letter to parents

Teaching and learning

14. Bloom's taxonomy
15. Make learning active
16. Lesson plan checklist
17. Good practice lesson observation (Appendix 4.2)
18. Short-term planning sheet – using the 'must, should, could' model
19. Differentiation PowerPoint presentation
20. Differentiation by content – curating a virtual exhibition
21. Medium-term planning sheet – incorporating a gallery visit
22. Organising a graphic design competition with a local business
23. IEP pro forma
24. Key art words

Unit of work on IDENTITY (Appendix 4.1)

25. IDENTITY – description and aims
26. IDENTITY – pupil activity sheets
27. IDENTITY – teacher checklist for evaluating progress
28. IDENTITY – work in focus and list of resources
29. Cindy Sherman background information

Images

All images used in this book, as well as further examples of student artwork, are included on the CD.

Highlights from the CD

Higher Ability Group
departmental procedure (2)

Enrichment opportunities for
developing talent in art (10)

Updating units of work in art
extension activities (11)

Evaluation tools (6)

Planning future provision (7)

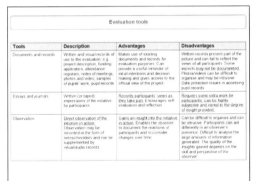

More able pupil nomination
sheet (12)

Sample letter to parents (13)

Bloom's taxonomy of learning
skills (14)

Lesson plan checklist (16)

Good practice lesson observation (17)

Differentiation (19)

Differentiation by content –
curating a virtual exhibition (20)

Individual education plan (IEP)
pro forma (23)

Checklist for evaluating
progress (27)

Introduction

Who should use this book?

This book is for all teachers of art working with Key Stage 3 and Key Stage 4 pupils. It will be relevant to teachers working within the full spectrum of schools, from highly selective establishments to comprehensive and secondary modern schools as well as some special schools. Its overall objective is to provide a practical resource that heads of department, gifted and talented coordinators and classroom teachers can use to develop a coherent approach to provision for their most able pupils.

Why is it needed?

School populations differ greatly and pupils considered very able in one setting might not stand out in another. Nevertheless, whatever the general level of ability within a school, there has been a tendency to plan and provide for the middle range, to modify for those who are struggling and to leave the most able to 'get on with it'. This has meant that the most able have:

- not been sufficiently challenged and stimulated

- underachieved

- been unaware of what they might be capable of achieving

- not had high enough ambitions and aspirations

- sometimes become disaffected.

How will this book help teachers?

This book and its accompanying CD will, through its combination of practical ideas, materials for photocopying or downloading, and case studies:

- help teachers of art to focus on the top 5–10% of the ability range in their particular school and to find ways of providing for these pupils, both within and beyond the classroom

- equip them with strategies and ideas to support exceptionally able pupils, i.e. those in the top 5% nationally.

Terminology

Since there is confusion about the meaning of the words 'gifted' and 'talented', the terms 'more able', 'most able' and 'exceptionally able' will generally be used in this series.

When 'gifted' and 'talented' are used, the definitions provided by the Department for Education and Skills (DfES) in its Excellence in Cities programme will apply. That is:

- **gifted** pupils are the most academically able in a school. This ability might be general or specific to a particular subject area, such as mathematics.

- **talented** pupils are those with high ability or potential in art, music, performing arts or sport.

The two groups together should form 5–10% of any school population.

There are, of course, some pupils who are both gifted and talented. Examples that come to mind are the budding physicist who plays the violin to a high standard in his spare time, or the pupil with high general academic ability who plays for the area football team.

This book is part of a series dealing with providing challenges for the most able secondary age pupils in a range of subjects. It is likely that some of the books in the series might also contain ideas that would be relevant to teachers of art.

CHAPTER 1

Our more able pupils – the national scene

- Making good provision for the more able – what's in it for schools?
- National initiatives since 1997
- LEA responsibilities to more able pupils
- School Ofsted inspections and more able pupils
- Some tools to support inspection and school development plans
- Other general support for teachers and parents of more able pupils

The purpose of this first chapter is to place the subject-specific content of all that follows into the more general national and school framework. It is easier to understand what needs to be done at departmental level if there is an appreciation of the context in which discussions are being made.

The debate about whether to make special provision for the most able pupils in secondary schools ran its course during the last decade of the twentieth century. Explicit provision to meet their learning needs is now considered neither elitist nor a luxury and, from an inclusion angle, these pupils must have the same chances as others to develop their potential to the full. But for teachers who are not convinced by the inclusion argument, there is a much more pragmatic reason for meeting the needs of able pupils. Quite simply, it is something that all teachers are now required to do, not an optional extra.

> All schools should seek to create an atmosphere in which to excel is not only acceptable but desirable.
>
> (*Excellence in Schools* – DfEE 1997)

> High achievement is determined by the school's commitment to inclusion and the steps it takes to ensure that every pupil does as well as possible.
>
> (*Handbook for Inspecting Secondary Schools* – Ofsted 2003)

A few years ago, efforts to raise standards in schools concentrated on getting as many pupils as possible over the Level 5 hurdle at the end of Key Stage 3 and over the five A*–C grades hurdle at GCSE. Resources were pumped into borderline pupils and the most able were not, on the whole, considered a cause for concern. The situation has changed dramatically in the last five years with schools being expected to set targets for A*s and As and to show added value by helping pupils entering the school with high SATs scores to achieve Levels 7 and beyond, if supporting data suggests that that is what they are capable of. Early recognition of high potential and the setting of curricular targets are at last addressing the lack of progress demonstrated by many able pupils in Year 7 and more attention is being paid to creating a climate in which learning can flourish. Nevertheless, there is a push for even more support for the most able through the promotion of personalised learning.

> The goal is that five years from now: gifted and talented students progress in line with their ability rather than their age; schools inform parents about tailored provision in an annual school profile; curricula include a gifted and talented dimension and at 14–19 there is more stretch and differentiation at the top-end, so no matter what your talent it will be engaged; and the effect of poverty on achievement is reduced, because support for high-ability students from poorer backgrounds enables them to thrive.
>
> (Speech at the National Academy for Gifted and Talented Youth – David Miliband, Minister of State for School Standards, May 2004)

It is hoped that this book, with the others in this series, will help to accelerate these changes.

Making good provision for the most able – what's in it for schools?

Schools and/or subject departments often approach provision for the most able pupils with some reluctance because they imagine a lot of extra work for very little reward. In fact, the rewards of providing for these pupils are substantial:

- It can be very stimulating to the subject specialist to explore ways of developing approaches with enthusiastic and able students.

> Taking a serious look at what I should expect from the most able and then at how I should teach them has given my teaching a new lease of life. I feel so sorry for youngsters who were taught by me 10 years ago. They must have been bored beyond belief. But then, to be quite honest, so was I.
>
> (Science teacher)

- Offering opportunities to tackle work in a more challenging manner often interests pupils whose abilities have gone unnoticed because they have not been motivated by a bland educational diet.

> Some of the others were invited to an after-school maths club. When I heard what they were doing, it sounded so interesting that I asked the maths teacher if I could go too. She was a bit doubtful at first because I

have messed about a lot but she agreed to take me on trial. I'm one of her star pupils now and she reckons I'll easily get an A*. I still find some of the lessons really slow and boring but I don't mess around – well, not too much.

(Year 10 boy)

- When pupils are engaged by the work they are doing, motivation, attainment and discipline improve.

    You don't need to be gifted to work out that the work we do is much more interesting and exciting. It's made others want to be like us.
    (Comment from a student involved in an extension programme for the most able)

- Schools that are identified as very good schools by Ofsted generally have good provision for their most able students.

    If you are willing to deal effectively with the needs of able pupils you will raise the achievement of all pupils.
    (Mike Tomlinson, former director of Ofsted)

- The same is true of individual departments in secondary schools. All those considered to be very good have spent time developing a sound working approach that meets the needs of their most able pupils.

    The department creates a positive atmosphere by its organisation, display and the way that students are valued. Learning is generally very good and often excellent throughout the school. The teachers' high expectations permeate the atmosphere and are a significant factor in raising achievement. These expectations are reflected in the curriculum which has depth and students are able and expected to experience difficult problems in all year groups.
    (Mathematics department, Hamstead Hall School, Birmingham; Ofsted 2003)

National initiatives since 1997

Since 1997, when the then Department for Education and Employment (DfEE) set up its Gifted and Talented Advisory Group, many initiatives designed to raise aspirations and levels of achievement have been targeted on the most able, especially in secondary schools. Currently, a three-pronged approach is in place, with:

1. special programmes, including Excellence in Cities, Excellence Clusters and Aimhigher, for areas of the country where educational standards in secondary schools are lowest

2. resources for teachers and pupils throughout the country, such as the National Academy for Gifted and Talented Youth, gifted and talented summer

schools, World Class Tests, National Curriculum Online and the G&TWISE website

3. regional support, which is currently confined to GATE A, in London.

1. Special programmes

Excellence in Cities

In an attempt to deal with the chronic underachievement of able pupils in inner city areas, Excellence in Cities (EiC) was launched in 1999. This is a very ambitious, well-funded programme with many different strands. It initially concentrated on secondary age pupils but work has been extended into the primary sector in many areas. 'Provision for the Gifted and Talented' is one of the strands.

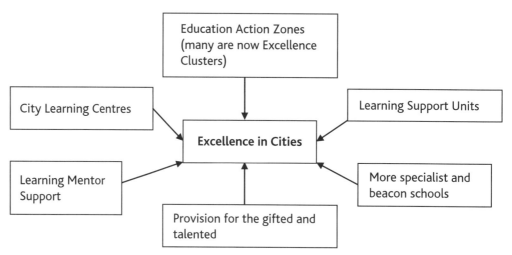

Strands in the Excellence in Cities initiatives

EiC schools are expected to:

- develop a whole-school policy for their most able pupils

- appoint a gifted and talented coordinator with sufficient time to fulfil the role

- send the coordinator on a national training programme run by Oxford Brookes University

- identify 5–10% of pupils in each year group as their gifted and talented cohort, the gifted being the academically able and the talented being those with latent or obvious ability in sport, music, art or the performing arts

- provide an appropriate programme of work both within the school day and beyond

- set 'aspirational' targets both for the gifted and talented cohort and for individual pupils

- work with other schools in a 'cluster' to provide further support for these pupils

- work with other agencies, such as Aimhigher, universities, businesses and private-sector schools, to enhance provision and opportunities for these pupils.

The influence of Excellence in Cities has stretched far beyond the areas where it is in place. There are a number of reasons for this:

- Partnership (LEA) gifted and talented coordinators set up regional support groups. These groups worked to raise awareness of the needs of these pupils and their teachers. One of the most successful is the Transpennine Group, which operates from Liverpool across to Hull. Early meetings concentrated on interpreting Department for Education and Skills (DfES) directives but later the group invited universities, support organisations, publishers and successful practitioners to share ideas with them. They also began to run activities for pupils across all the EiC partnerships involved. By constantly feeding back information from the meetings to the DfES, it began to have some influence on policy. Teachers and advisers outside EiC areas have adopted similar models and the DfES is now funding regional support groups that include both EiC and non-EiC areas.

- Publishers have responded to demand from gifted and talented coordinators and are producing more materials, both books and software, that challenge the most able.

- Some LEAs have worked with Oxford Brookes University to extend their coordinator training into non-EiC areas.

- **The requirements of EiC schools have come to be regarded as a blueprint for all secondary schools.** The DfES guidance for EiC schools is available for all schools at www.standards.dfes.gov.uk/giftedandtalented.

Excellence Clusters

Although EiC was set up initially in the main urban conurbations, other hotspots of underachievement and poverty have since been identified and Excellence Clusters have been established. For example, Ellesmere Port, Crewe and Barrow-in-Furness are pockets of deprivation, with major social problems and significant underachievement, in otherwise affluent areas. Excellence Clusters have been established in these three places and measures are being taken to improve provision for the most able pupils.

Aimhigher

There have been a number of changes in EiC over the years. One of the most recent is that, in secondary schools, the EiC programme now supports the most able between the ages of 11 and 14, but from 14 to 19 their needs are met through Aimhigher, another initiative of the DfES. Its remit is to widen participation in UK higher education, particularly among students from groups that do not have a tradition of going to university, such as ethnic minorities, the disabled and those from poorer homes. Support for these pupils begins while they are still in school and includes:

- activities in schools and colleges to encourage them and raise their aspirations

- extra money to universities to enable them to provide summer schools and outreach work with pupils

- The Young People's Publicity Campaign providing information and advice to those from disadvantaged backgrounds

financial support for students through 26,000 Opportunity Bursaries worth £2,000 each over three years for young people.

The Aimhigher website is at www.aimhigher.ac.uk.

2. Resources for teachers and pupils throughout the country

National Academy for Gifted and Talented Youth

Government initiatives for the most able pupils have not been confined to those in deprived areas. In 2002, the National Academy for Gifted and Talented Youth was established at Warwick University. Its brief is to offer support to the most able 5% of the school population and to their teachers and parents, and it is doing this in a number of ways.

The National Academy for Gifted and Talented Youth		
Student Academy	Professional Academy	Expertise Centre
• Summer schools, including link-ups with the Center for Talented Youth (CTY) in the USA • Outreach courses in a wide range of subjects at universities and other venues across the country • Online activities – currently maths, classics, ethics and philosophy	• Continuing professional development (CPD) for teachers • A PGCE+ programme for trainee teachers • Ambassador School Programme to disseminate good practice amongst schools	• Leading research in gifted and talented education

Bursaries are available for pupils from low-income families so that they are not denied access to the activities. The Academy's website is at www.nagty.ac.uk.

Gifted and talented summer schools

Each LEA is provided with money to run a number of summer schools (dependent on the size of the authority) for the most able pupils in Years 6–9. The approach to the selection and management of these schools differs from area to area. For example, some authorities organise them centrally while others allow schools to bid to run one of the summer schools. The main aim obviously is to challenge and stimulate these pupils but the DfES also hopes that:

- the summer schools will encourage teachers and advisers to adopt innovative teaching approaches

- teachers will continue to monitor these pupils over time

- where Year 6 pupils are involved, it will make secondary teachers aware of what they can achieve and raise their expectations of Year 7 pupils.

More can be found out about these summer schools at: www.standards.dfes. gov.uk/giftedandtalented/. Unfortunately, direct funding from the DfES for summer schools ceased in 2005.

World Class Tests

These have been introduced by the Qualifications and Curriculum Authority (QCA) to allow schools to judge the performance of their most able pupils against national and international standards. Tests are currently available for 9- and 13-year-olds in mathematics and problem solving. Some schools have found that the problem solving tests are effective at identifying able underachievers in maths and science. The website, at www.worldclassarena.org.uk, contains sample questions so that teachers, parents and pupils themselves can assess the tests' suitability for particular pupils or groups of pupils.

National Curriculum Online

The National Curriculum Online website, administered by QCA, provides general guidance on all aspects of the National Curriculum but also has a substantial section on general and subject-specific issues relating to gifted and talented education, including identification strategies, case studies, management and units of work. The website is at www.nc.uk.net/gt.

G&TWISE

The G&TWISE website has recently replaced the one called Xcalibre. It links to recommended resources for gifted and talented pupils, checked by professionally qualified subject editors, in all subjects and at all Key Stages. It is part-funded by the Gifted and Talented Education Unit of the DfES. The website is at www2. teachernet.gov.uk/gat/.

3. Regional support

At this stage, regional support is confined to GATE A, a branch of London Challenge. Four London EiC partnerships have collaborated with universities, cultural centres and professional bodies to develop a coordinated approach to supporting the most able pupils throughout the region.

Central to this is the MLE or Managed Learning Environment, which provides pupils with interactive learning materials. Some key features of this include:

- video conferencing and online alerts for specific groups of users

- online assignments and tests

- course calendars and linked personal calendars

- personal study records.

GATE A provides five 'Student Learning Pathways' so that the approach can be matched to a student's stage of development and needs. There are subject, themed and cross-curricular skills-based pathways as well as one directed at Aimhigher students, and one for work-related learning. The initiative also strives to support the parents and carers of more able pupils. The website is at www.londongt.org.

The initiatives discussed above do not include the many subject specific developments, such as those from QCA, that have taken place during this period. These will be dealt with in later chapters.

LEA responsibilities to more able pupils

Schools and departments should not be shy of approaching their LEA for help when developing their more able pupil provision. Local authorities, as well as schools, are expected to support more able pupils and schools can and should turn to them for support and advice.

The notes from Ofsted on LEA Link Inspection published in December 2003 state that the main tasks of LEAs, with regard to offering support to schools for gifted and talented pupils, are:

- to provide guidance to schools in meeting pupils' needs

- to identify schools which need particular help and to ensure that this is provided effectively

- where appropriate, to support initiatives across the LEA, such as gifted and talented summer schools, Excellence in Cities, Excellence Clusters and helping pupils to access resources such as the National Academy for Gifted and Talented Youth

- to support individual pupils with particular talents in order that they make progress

- to learn lessons from Excellence in Cities areas.

After a period when many LEAs did very little to support these pupils in a systematic manner, the climate has now changed and many have taken measures such as:

- producing gifted and talented guidelines for schools

- running continuing professional development (CPD) programmes, sometimes with the help of Oxford Brookes University, which provide training for EiC gifted and talented coordinators

- encouraging federations of local schools to work together to make additional provision for the most able

- setting up masterclasses and advanced learning centres

- identifying good practice in schools and disseminating this to other schools in the authority.

Ofsted – expectations of secondary schools

The most able must be seen to have as many opportunities for development as other pupils. Poor, unchallenging teaching or an ideology that confuses equality of opportunity with levelling down must not hinder their progress. The environment for learning should be one in which it is safe to be clever or to excel.

Throughout the new Ofsted *Handbook for Inspecting Secondary Schools* (2003), there are both direct and indirect references to schools' responsibilities to their most able pupils. Wherever the phrase 'all pupils should . . .' appears in this handbook, teachers need to ask themselves not only how this applies to pupils with special educational needs (SEN) and other disadvantaged groups but also how this applies to their most able pupils.

A summary of some of the more important points relating to more able pupils from this handbook is included in Appendix 1.1, where page numbers are provided so that teachers can find out more.

Some tools to support inspection and school development plans

In light of the above, teachers might find the Pre-Ofsted checklist on the next page and the National Quality Standards in Gifted and Talented Education (Appendix 1.2) helpful either when preparing for Ofsted or when looking into developing this area of work as part of the school development plan. More about national quality standards in gifted and talented education can be found at www.standards.dfes.gov.uk/giftedandtalented/strategyandstrands.

It is important to remember that:

- the development of provision for the more able should be firmly enmeshed with other curricular and pastoral strategies and should fit in to the overall school philosophy

- classroom practice should match school and departmental policy.

Other general support for teachers and parents of more able pupils

Two organisations which must be included when there is any mention of support for more able pupils, their teachers and parents are NACE and NAGC.

NACE

The National Association for Able Children in Education, or NACE as it is generally known, is primarily a support organisation for teaching professionals. It has many publications on the education of more able pupils, many of them produced in association with David Fulton Publishers. Its Challenge Award has been particularly well received. Conferences are regularly held around the country and training can be provided at school, LEA or regional level. It can also provide consultancy tailored to the individual needs of schools. The Association's website is at www.nace.co.uk.

	Pre-Ofsted able pupil checklist	✓
1.	Does the school have a policy for its most able pupils?	
2.	Is there a school coordinator for the most able?	
3.	Is there someone in each department with whom the coordinator can liaise?	
4.	Are there identification strategies in place that are understood by all?	
5.	Do these strategies identify both academic ability and talent in specific areas of the curriculum?	
6.	Does the balance of the most able cohort match the school profile in terms of gender, ethnicity and social class?	
7.	Do pupils' achievements match their potential taking into account the school's performance data and other evidence?	
8.	Is negative stereotyping of the most able challenged?	
9.	Do teachers support the most able with: – high expectations?	
10.	– the employment of a wide range of teaching styles?	
11.	– a suitable pace?	
12	– extension and enrichment activities?	
13.	– the selection of suitable resources?	
14.	Does the school's organisation of pupils into groups and sets take account the needs of these pupils?	
15.	Does the school have an appropriate curriculum for the most able?	
16.	Do pupils have access to any of the following: learning mentors; study support; out-of-school activities; masterclasses; specialists; resources in other schools and colleges?	
17.	Are senior managers alert to the need to monitor and track the progress of the most able?	
18.	Is suitable training for staff arranged when the need arises?	
19.	Do senior managers take action when the needs of the most able are not being met?	
20.	Are the most able pupils positive about the education and support they receive in the school?	
21.	Are parents content with school provision?	

NAGC

The focus of the National Association for Gifted Children is primarily on the children themselves although it does offer support to parents and teachers as well. It can offer:

- branches throughout the country where children with similar interests or abilities can meet at regular intervals

- online activities for 3- to 10-year-olds

- counselling for young people and parents

- support through its Youth Agency for 11- to 20-year-olds with web pages to which they have exclusive access

- INSET

- publications.

The Association's website is at www.nagcbritain.org.uk.

Summary

- Schools must provide suitable challenge and appropriate support for their most able pupils.
- Appropriate provision can enhance motivation and improve behaviour.
- There are many agencies that can help teachers with this work.
- LEAs, as well as schools, have a duty to support the education of more able pupils.
- Ofsted teams expect to see suitable provision for the most able. It is an inclusion issue.
- School policy, with regard to more able children, must be reflected in practice.

Departmental policy and approach

It is a widely held belief that the responsibility for the education of able children rests not solely in the hands of the head of department, the gifted and talented coordinator or the headteacher of a school – it is the responsibility of every teacher and member of support staff as all are responsible for the education of the whole child.

> For a school to be truly effective in its provision for able children it will need to consider provision for the most able as a feature of every aspect of the school.
>
> (Eyre 1997)

However, on an individual level, it usually falls to a named member of every department in a Secondary School to ensure that provision for the able child is, for example, discussed at departmental meetings, that subject-specific INSET is undertaken and disseminated to the rest of the department, that monitoring and evaluation are regularly checked. With this in mind, the following considerations may wish to be made and will be looked at within this chapter:

- the role of the subject/department leader

- a departmental policy

- an audit of current provision/action plan

- acceleration/fast tracking

- resources

- liaison with other departments

- individual education plans

- INSET.

Role of the subject or department leader or person with responsibility for more able pupils in art

As a subject leader, you will ultimately have responsibility for the quality of the teaching and learning in your department. You, or the person with responsibility for able pupils in your department, could:

- Start by identifying and acknowledging good practice that already exists.

- Identify any gaps in provision/expertise and research subject-specific/able pupils INSET opportunities; disseminate all information to members of the art department after the event – theory and practice should go hand-in-hand.

- Ensure that all staff in your department are aware of those children who are particularly able in one or more areas of art, craft or design and that their names are highlighted on all registers. Note: often a child's oral contribution during discussions around an artist's work or the development and ideas around their own and others' work can flag up an otherwise unnoticed ability in the subject, particularly if they are not as able practically. This talent should also be recognised.

- Ensure that schemes of work and lesson plans are suitably differentiated to provide a range of learning opportunities that cater for the needs of the more able or indeed, allow opportunities to discover new talents (remember 'Billy Elliot'!).

- Ensure that the art department is resourced with a wide and varied selection of specialist materials and equipment – as far as funding will allow – or that staff and pupils know where they can access resources outside the department. Resources should also include a selection of books, CDs, DVDs or videos to extend learning on art movements, artists, craftspeople and designers from the past right up to the present day – again, the range offered will depend on the departmental budget allocated. For those schools that benefit from specific gifted and talented funding in EiC areas, these resources could be 'bid for' through the internal school system. **It is highly advisable to review and evaluate the resources used on a regular basis in order to assess effective impact on pupils' learning.** Perhaps this could be done prior to the new financial year and before orders for new materials are placed.

- Ensure that out-of-school-hours activities organised by your department have a suitable proportion of time allocated to the extension of classroom activities and that they are also differentiated for the more able child. This could allow a child to explore a topic in more breadth and depth, to experiment with materials or research other artists, or to allow for more one-to-one guidance. Art departments have a history of providing such opportunities so this will be nothing new to you! This type of activity is called 'study support' and it may be worth asking the senior management team in your school if there is any external funding available to help your department in providing these out-of-school-hours sessions, for example to provide extra materials.

- Ensure that the progress of the more able child in art is monitored in order to sustain progress and that departmental planning is reviewed and evaluated, updating if necessary, on a regular basis.

A departmental policy

Schools should have a whole-school policy that is either specifically about its provision for more able pupils or explicitly highlights able pupils in its general one. It is also good practice for each subject department to have its own departmental policy that is brief but discusses specific provision and opportunities for its able pupils. Often schools provide each department with an outline for a generic policy that can be easily adapted to suit the subject area. Departmental policies are needed to ensure consistency of approach by all staff and to highlight the vision for the provision for able pupils in your department. This is particularly helpful to NQTs, new members of staff or those on short-term contracts and parents. Your department may also be involved in supporting PGCE or BEd students from a local university and by giving them access to the policy you will extend their knowledge and understanding of differentiated provision. Ultimately, able pupils have an educational 'need' – their learning should be an equal opportunities consideration just as much as any other pupil. It is the responsibility of all who enter your department to meet those needs to the best of their ability by being as fully informed as possible.

The first part of the policy should include a rationale and discuss what the department feels high ability in art and design might actually look like. This part of the document may be written following time spent analysing 'Able in art means . . .' during INSET days or at the very least, departmental meetings. Identification will be looked at in more detail in the next chapter.

See Appendix 2.1 for an outline policy based on that from the art department at St Aelred's Catholic Technology College in St Helens, Merseyside (with kind permission of Kevin Kelly, head of art). This policy can be adapted to your own department's use and is included as a Word document on the accompanying CD. The sub-headings cover all the main areas of concern but you may wish to go into more specific detail if you already have established good procedures in place. Do bear in mind, however, that the policy should be reviewed and updated on a yearly basis and some elements may change due to unforeseen circumstances, such as a specialism no longer being offered within the department owing to staff changes, etc.

Audit of current provision and action planning

Basic audits will establish what is already in place within a department. However, these can be added to in order, for example, to assess the impact of provision upon pupil results. Audits are not very appealing but they are a great way of benchmarking and assessing ways forward for the department. Appendix 2.2 contains a generic audit for heads of department to get an overview of current provision for able pupils. Schools who have used this tool have found it a useful precursor to drafting a departmental action plan – a pro forma for this is also included as Appendix 2.3. Both are on the accompanying CD.

The secret to successful action planning is to set achievable targets with elements of challenge built in. This is to try to ensure progress is made and that the progress is measurable, especially when thinking about the impact upon exam results in your subject.

But we must not forget about those 'soft' targets that cannot be measured in the same way, such as the improvement in a child's confidence in experimenting with new methods or materials, or the way in which they express themselves verbally. We should not automatically assume that all able pupils are confident and articulate! A child may be, for example, a perfectionist who is an excellent recorder of detailed direct observations but when asked to try new materials, different approaches and so on may 'freeze' rather than be seen to 'fail' or not appear to be as good at this as he/she is at other things. Short, written statements could be kept by teachers or support staff in registers alongside pupil names when progress in these areas is made and perhaps the work done by these pupils at that time could be kept in a portfolio or photographs taken in order to make a more 'formal' recording of the progress.

Acceleration or fast tracking

In this context, acceleration or fast tracking means that a pupil or a cohort of pupils can move rapidly through a course, say for example, GCSE Art and Design being taken in Year 9 or 10 instead of Year 11. It could also mean that a pupil actually moves through the whole of their schooling in advance of their years, working with older children, due to their high ability.

Fast tracking a whole cohort is often a better option from the teacher's point of view as they can plan ahead for pupils to go from GCSE to A level work, to following a university-level course. This does however rely upon good communication routes to access the higher-level courses and may be very time-consuming, especially in an 11–16 school. Pupils should only be fast tracked if it is in their best interests and perhaps in most cases, schools would argue that long-term benefits were dubious.

On an individual pupil basis, fast tracking may be more appropriate but timetables would need to be managed carefully. For example, it may be feasible to allow a Year 9 able artist to work with a Year 10 or 11 option group on the GCSE Art course and be in the rest of her lessons with her peers. Any missed subjects that the pupils would normally do in this time though would need to be made up out-of-hours in order to meet National Curriculum requirements. This is, in practice, a rarely used strategy. In most cases it is preferable to offer the pupil the chance to study the subject in more breadth and depth rather than move them towards the next exam more quickly. The child must be mature and able to cope emotionally with all that fast tracking involves. The debate continues . . .

Allocation of resources

As mentioned previously, it is essential that able pupils have access to their fair share of resources relating to a subject area. Within art and design this may mean that they can experiment with materials that are a bit 'different' such as silk paints, screen printing equipment or breezeblocks for carving. But it may also mean that they are allowed to use traditional materials in a broader, newer sense – trying different types of paint such as oil, acrylic, etc. and applying them to a range of surfaces for a range of purposes. This is nothing new – it is offering a broad and balanced curriculum, whilst building-in challenge.

In the same way, giving able pupils access to a variety of research materials will enhance critical study skills, allowing them to evaluate and reflect on the work of others in greater depth. Books that are too simple in their format will not allow for this and may mean that learning plateaus. The teacher should guide them through the work of perhaps less well-known artists, craftspeople and designers in order to suitably extend their learning in a particular field, genre or specialism. For example, if an art department has internet access it may wish to use websites such as the National Gallery of Washington DC (www.nga.gov) which has an interactive section 'ngakids' for children, which would particularly suit able Year 7 pupils who wish to extend their critical study skills in fun ways. The activities on the website change on a regular basis, allowing the site to be used in class or during extension/out-of-hours activities throughout the year.

Liaison with other departments

Working with other departments in the school is always a beneficial way of sharing practice between teachers and support staff but it is also a good way of showing pupils how transferable some skills can be. Often art departments may work with design and technology departments, most commonly textiles, so that the skills learned in each of those subjects can benefit higher quality coursework and sketchbook or portfolio work as elements of Key Stage 3 and GCSE requirements are very similar. Just as easily, the elements of composition, imagination, creativity, expressing feelings and exploring issues and ideas can be linked to the subjects of English language and literature, history and PSHE, amongst others.

The following case study highlights an example of cross-departmental working (design and technology and art departments) with more able pupils. It is reproduced here with kind permission of the author, Sue Buckley, senior design and technology teacher at St Augustine's Catholic High School, St Helens. It also features on the DfES Standards site as an example of good practice: www.standards.dfes.gov.uk/giftedandtalented/goodpractice/cs/gcseart

GCSE Art for talented pupils

What was it like before the work and why was the work undertaken?

The aim of the project was to provide workshops for GCSE Art students with a high level of skill in basic techniques but with little experience in developing a single piece of work into a variety of media. Many of the students in the group also studied GCSE Textiles Technology, an area the art teacher wished to develop within the art department.

The group included a number of less well-motivated students and those with little support outside school.

The experience had to be something that would grasp their imagination and motivate them sufficiently to work independently. The students had some knowledge of individual artists and their work.

It was decided that the work would best be presented by an artist who would be credible and was known to be capable of working with students of this age group.

What was planned?

The professional partnership 'ART' was approached and pre-meetings were arranged so that the needs of the sessions were fully discussed.

'ART' is a joint venture. Pat Southern, former art adviser in Lancashire, and her partner Julian have been working together to provide workshops for several years. Staff from St Augustine's have attended these workshops and have always been delighted with the standard of preparation and the delivery as well as the success of the pupils.

It was decided that the work of Gustav Klimt would be the focus as it would lend itself to development in a wide variety of media, particularly textiles.

Two consecutive days were identified:

- Day 1: Students to be presented with a variety of developmental tasks, prepared resource and worksheets to support them in developing a number of individual pieces of work to complete GCSE coursework by the end of the day.
- Day 2: Consolidate the work and think about how to develop it into at least one media piece.

Day 2 was planned for a Saturday so that the more motivated students would attend and succeed in the second part of the task.

What was done and when?

Two staff were taken off timetable for the day; staff from other high schools were invited to attend. Two technology staff from Rainford High School came to the Friday session and voluntarily worked with groups of students and completed some tasks themselves. They were given sets of the photocopied materials to take back with them to use in their own lessons.

The artists brought a large variety of materials for the students to work with which really excited the students.

- **Activity 1:** The approach was to start small to build confidence. The group were taught the techniques of selection of motif, bold drawing skills and presentation of work through other artists' work. The most popular with the group was Rizzi. His graffiti-like approach to people and buildings in New York was inspiring.
- **Activity 2:** The work of Klimt was introduced to the group by which time they were used to selecting and analysing.
- **Activity 3:** The final session of Day 1 was to look at the written content of some of Klimt's work and the writing styles of the late 19th and early 20th centuries. Samples of writing that had been prepared in advance were handed out and the students sent home to practice.

Day 2 was to start a little later (it was Saturday!). However, some students were so keen that they were there when we opened!

Day 2 was optional and only two students did not attend. These were two who we felt would have been the least likely to have completed their homework. The rest had produced an amazing amount of work and were familiar with the styles of writing and were able to reproduce them quite easily.

The final large pieces of work were begun. These would be multi-media, the first being a collage, the second worked on MDF – a material that none of the students had worked with before.

The day followed a similar pattern to the first day with continual encouragement and suggestions from the artists. The most difficult part of the day was getting the students to stop! By the time the students left, staff had put up their work from the two days in displays covering all the entrance halls to school.

What has been the impact and how was it verified?

The immediate impact that these workshops had was in the enthusiasm with which the students spoke of their experiences to other students and to staff. This had an effect on their attitude in art lessons – some students had now been reassured of their talent – others had an improved attitude realising the amount of preparation that goes into a successful piece of work. The full impact was seen in their GCSE results in 2004, which were excellent!

Within the school the resources have been used with Years 9, 10 and 11, in art and in textiles. It has enabled students to see the links between the two subject areas and has given staff the opportunity to work collaboratively. The techniques used in the delivery of the sessions have also been used in class successfully.

What has been learnt and next steps?

This proved to be a most successful activity. Using professionals or experts in their field is essential for more able students. Showing them the best helps to bring out the best.

Using adults other than teachers is most beneficial. This will be continued in both the art and textiles departments and encouraged within the rest of the school.

Excellent organisation is essential for all activities. This not only enables activities and events to run smoothly but also demonstrates the need for good organisation to the students.

Timing of events is essential. Teachers should look at schemes of work and the school calendar to place the activity correctly where it will have the most impact. Our decision was to allow students to settle into the GCSE courses but to gain the most from the skills learned the event had to be quite early in the courses.

We will not run an identical event again – staff feel that they were sufficiently trained by taking part and they can now deliver this particular workshop themselves. However, staff will use adults other than teachers again to help deliver part of the curriculum.

Staff are already using the skills learned with other groups and will continue to do so. Evidence of the skills can be seen in students' work in a number of different subject areas. The presentation of their work has improved and they are now using their newfound handwriting techniques to annotate work instead of the computer. For creative work, the hand method is much more flexible.

This case study is a working example of what can be achieved in a short space of time with the correct provision, pace, level of activity and depth and breadth of experience. Funding for this particular project came from the gifted and talented budget in the school as part of EiC but subsequent events have been planned for and incorporated from general departmental capitation budgets as a means of enriching the curriculum in cross-curricular ways.

The heads of department internal audit, featured earlier in the chapter, may be a sound starting point in looking at the ways each department

provides for their most able pupils. By collating the findings, departments can be linked together to work on joint projects, share ideas, deliver informal INSET to each other, share resources or identify training needs. This process may need to be done by senior management or the school's able pupils coordinator, but it allows for more focused ways forward in order for children to benefit from perhaps, a joined-up way of working where departments share similar aims and objectives.

Individual education plans

For able pupils, individual education plans (IEPs) are subject-specific target-setting sheets that are a means of challenging them more specifically and monitoring their progress. There is a lot of debate about this process – if we target-set through IEPs for the more able, and have more detailed IEPs for pupils with Special Educational Needs, what are we doing for those pupils in-between? Do we set individual targets for all our pupils? Does this have any impact on pupil learning? How do we know? In cases where schools do this for able pupils through departments, the results are mixed. If there are sufficient staff who are given the task of monitoring this progress, and it is not just the responsibility of the school's able pupils coordinator, IEPs have been proven to work extremely well in raising attainment and achievement. Where the responsibility lies solely with one person, the task has proved unmanageable.

Below (and on the accompanying CD) is an example of an IEP that will fit onto a side of A4. It should be a working document, agreed and signed by the pupil, subject teacher and parent or guardian as a way of ensuring its importance within the teaching and learning of the child.

This format can be adapted to suit any department in a school. IEPs may be completed once per term, during any available time, possibly as part of the art lesson with a small group of pupils. They should be given guidance on what a meaningful target is and should be allowed time to reflect on the areas they may wish to improve in. In other words, targets such as 'remember to bring my sketchbook to lessons' aren't particularly motivating or specific enough. It would be better to identify a skill area that can be improved such as 'in my observation work, I must try using a range of pencils – 2B, 4B, etc. – to improve my use of tone'.

A review date has been incorporated on this pro forma and this should normally be at the start of the following term, thus keeping paperwork to a minimum as targets are only set and reviewed three times in the academic year. If insufficient progress has been made, the same target may be set again the following term; however, this should not go on indefinitely as the pupil will lose interest and lose sight of the goal he is aiming for. It is highly advisable for subject teachers to review the individual targets for able pupils, as they know best what is required.

Again, this process should be tried out first with a small group of identified able artists to assess whether or not it will be beneficial to pupils and is manageable for teaching staff. A starting point may be a group of able Year 10

School Name

Able Pupils Individual Education Plan for Art and Design

Autumn Term 2005

Name of pupil: ....

Form/Year group: ....

Summary of background evidence of higher ability in art and design:

Targets set for this term:

1. ....

2. ....

3. ....

Review date: ....

(Spring term 2006) Comments on progress made:

Signed (pupil): ....

Signed (teacher): ....

Signed (parent/guardian): ....

Date: ....

pupils and the impact of IEPs can be monitored against GCSE results in other subject areas, or just within art and design – monitoring progress against predicted grades and actual grades in the subject. Teachers should bear in mind however, that some pupils may not wish to have attention drawn to them in this way and may 'opt out' of the process. This has happened in a minority of cases.

INSET activities

We all know how precious time is during whole-school INSET days – they never seem to happen often enough and they're planned so far in advance that you may be looking into the next decade before you get the chance to work as a whole staff on the provision for able pupils! But most schools allocate specific time during these days for departmental working either on a given theme or an area of the department's own choice. The following suggestions could be activities that are carried out during these times or during normal departmental meetings as the need arises. At some point during the school year, provision for able pupils in every department should be looked at in detail. Here are some ideas with all PowerPoint presentations reproduced on the accompanying CD for your adaptation and use:

● what we mean by 'able in art and design' and identification of talented pupils

● enrichment opportunities for developing talent in art

● updating units of work to ensure they allow for full differentiation and extension activities.

What do we mean by
'Able' in Art and Design at
Key Stages 3 and 4?

Activity 1

(20 minutes)

Individually:

➤ Select one class that you teach from Key Stage 3 and Key Stage 4

➤ Try to identify one or more talented artists in each Key Stage

➤ What characteristics or criteria do you use to identify such pupils?

Activity 2

(20 minutes)

As a group:

➤ Compare your criteria with others in your department

➤ Sort the criteria under subheadings: *Drawing and Painting, 3D, Textiles, Graphics and ICT, Critical Study Skills, Print* and write each on a different coloured piece of paper or card.

Activity 3

(20 minutes)

As a group:

➤ Look at the list of identification strategies listed in *Chapter 3* of the book that accompanies this CD

➤ Compare your lists with this one and discuss any amendments, additions, etc., to try to come with as definitive a list for each subheading as you can.

Activity 4

➤ Over the next 2 weeks, compile a list of pupils who you now consider to be able in Art. Try to keep to between 5–10% of the number of pupils in each class that you teach individually – if there are none, this is fine!

➤ Hand the lists in to the Head of Department. At a suitable point, work as a department to compile one list of able pupils for each year group that is roughly 5–10% of the total number in that year group.

Activity 5

➤ Now you have your 'Able Pupils in Art' list for each year group, ensure that their names are highlighted in all your registers.

➤ Plan a time when you will work on the next step: PROVISION

INSET activity: What do we mean by 'able' in art and design at Key Stages 3 and 4?

Enrichment Opportunities for Developing Talent in Art, Craft and Design

Discussion

(10 minutes)

Enrichment activities have particular advantages:

➢ Longer than lesson time, allowing for more depth of experience.

➢ Vertically organised. So, for example, younger pupils learn from older ones.

➢ Participants come into contact with professional artists and skilled specialist teachers.

➢ All participants share a common high motivation for the subject.

Activity 1

(10 minutes)

➢ Under each of the previous bullet points, suggest specific examples that might feasibly be incorporated into lesson planning/year planning for the next academic year in Art, such as after-school clubs, gallery visits to specific exhibitions, etc.

Activity 2

(20 minutes)

➢ Now discuss as a group how these will directly impact upon the learning of more able pupils in Art and what can be built into these activities so that they are fully differentiated.

Activity 3

(10 minutes)

➢ Refer back to the original list of the advantages of enrichment activities.

➢ How many of these have you incorporated? Can you include any more?

INSET activity: Enrichment opportunities for developing talent in art, craft and design

Updating Units of Work in Art

Extension Activities

Activity 1

(30 minutes)

Look at one of your Units of Work in Art.

How can it be adapted for:

✓ Increased pace

✓ Increased depth

✓ Increased breadth

✓ Out-of-school opportunities

✓ Extension work/differentiated homework

Activity 2

(30 minutes)

Look at one of your Units of Work in Art.

Suggest specific Art activities for inclusion of the following EXTENSION activities:

✓ Increased use of ICT

✓ Evaluation of own work

✓ Mentoring of younger pupils by older ones

✓ Direction and rehearsal (e.g. Extra guidance, planning and preparation)

✓ Making comparisons with other artists in the same genre

✓ Synthesis activities (e.g. Categorising, combining, compiling, composing, designing, planning and revising)

Activity 3

(over the next 4 weeks)

➢ Update and adapt your Units of Work for the next academic year to ensure they are now fully differentiated to cater for your more able pupils in Art in all years.

➢ Adapt these Units to include specific extension activities

INSET activity: Updating units of work in art extension activities

Recognising high ability and potential

This chapter will consider what we mean by high ability and how we identify it in the pupils we teach in art and design. We touched on some identification strategies in the previous chapter but will now also look at other specific strategies. Once a child's abilities have been recognised, teachers' planning can be informed. Above all, schools should be inclusive in their identification rather than exclusive, and bear in mind the saying 'a rising tide floats all ships' – provide for the more able and the attainment and achievement of **all** pupils will rise.

Identification strategies

The Gifted and Talented Initiative through Excellence in Cities has sometimes been felt to be exclusive as the DfES prescribed a cohort of five to ten per cent of pupils on roll in a school to be identified for monitoring purposes as either 'gifted' (in 'academic' subjects such as maths, English, science, etc.) or 'talented' (in the subjects of art, music, drama, dance, PE and sport) with a seven per cent gifted and three per cent talented split. For some staff, this 'exclusivity' has not appeared to fit in with the 'comprehensive' ideal but the focus has remained on this percentage over the past three years or so. In practice, all EiC schools have identified 'shadow' cohorts (i.e. up to ten per cent of pupils particularly able in a specific subject in each year group) and many, many more students have benefited from specific provision than the 'official' five to ten per cent.

The more strategies used for identifying able pupils, the better. This allows teachers to find out information about their pupils that perhaps they did not know and leaves less opportunity for missing something. In secondary schools, it is important that teachers share information across all subjects both formally (test data, etc.) and informally, in conversation in the staffroom or after a parents' evening, for example. Test data may play a part in identification, but in art and design there are many much more imaginative and inclusive ways of recognising ability and spotting potential, as the subject is so wide-ranging and varied, covering many disciplines and skill areas. Evidence may be gathered from any of the following and should be used in a broad and balanced way when identifying a cohort of artistically able pupils.

Transition from Key Stage 2 to 3

It is a well-known fact that unfortunately fewer and fewer teachers are entering the profession at primary level with an arts specialist background. Although many higher education institutions that run BA and PGCE courses are currently looking at ways of addressing this, primary colleagues with a specialist art and design background are a bit thin on the ground. At the same time, local education authorities seem to be gradually changing art advisory roles into general adviser roles and support for the primary art curriculum can sometimes be lost. In the North West of England, advisers and consultants have established the 'arts entitlement before enrichment strategy'. This was originally set up by Cheshire LEA and Arts Council England North West, to address the concerns of 'quality' and 'quantity' in the primary classroom by linking primary with secondary colleagues and 'entitlement strategy' leaders based at the LEAs. The strategy was a response to primary colleagues wanting the best art and design (and other arts) provision for their children but not sure how to go about it, or indeed, knowing what quality provision might look like. Various strategies have been used to assist them in this:

● by working within or towards the Artsmark framework as a quantative starting point

● holding INSET activities (some led by art and design advanced skills teachers), activities with their local secondary school art departments

- specifically designed projects that bring practising artists into primaries to work with children while non-specialist teachers observe, learn, practise and team-teach alongside them.

The impact of such activities has significantly contributed to the quality and quantity of artistic provision within a number of primaries in the space of less than a year (2004–5) and has raised confidence in the non-specialist to tackle a range of art practices. On a smaller scale, this could be done by individual secondary art departments and their feeder primaries. Joint INSET, activity days and summer schools have been extremely successful in helping departments identify able Year 6 pupils who will be coming to them the following September. A simpler idea for transition in art and design from Key Stage 2 to 3 can be to ask all Year 6 teachers from feeder primaries to keep a portfolio of their children's artwork completed that year and allow them to bring it with them to their new secondary school in the September. Secondary teachers can then make their own judgements from what they see before implementing identification strategies and projects of their own if needed. Portfolios can be accompanied by short statements from Year 6 teachers on the pupils' particular strengths, enthusiasm, preferred learning styles and personal interests – after all, this can only assist in the ease of transition of pupils at a time when they are often worried and very apprehensive about starting a new school. Any artwork that can be on display when new Year 7s come into the art room for the first time can prove to be very reassuring.

Teacher nomination

As an experienced teacher you know how your pupils perform best in your lessons and you know what and how they ought to be achieving for their age and/or ability. Evidence should be collected objectively however and consideration should be given to those pupils who are perhaps not 'outwardly' expressive of their ability such as pupils with SEN, those who use English as an additional language or those who are merely quiet or untidy in the presentation of their work. Teachers can become aware of the abilities of their pupils through a range of activities which take place in the normal course of lessons such as:

- observing them at work in lessons

- setting them varied tasks that require them to utilise many different skills

- listening to their responses to questions – particularly those requiring them to analyse, synthesise and evaluate (Bloom's higher order thinking skills)

- discussing with them how they learn best and what they enjoy/dislike

- the progress they are making.

But sometimes as subject specialists, we have a gut-instinct, especially about those pupils who could potentially be really talented in art. This should not be ignored even though it is certainly less easy to record on paper!

Once identified, the information suggested below could be used by subject teachers to record nominations in order to assist in the drawing-up of individual education plans (discussed in Chapter 2) for example:

a. name of pupil and class/year group

b. area(s) of ability within art, craft and design

c. specific evidence which has led you to identifying this pupil

d. next steps for this pupil which may be included on an IEP

e. date of nomination and name of teacher.

This should fit onto a side of A4, no more, and may look like the following example:

School Name

More Able Pupil in Art and Design

Nomination Sheet

Name of pupil: ....

Form/Year group: ....

Area(s) of particular ability in art, craft and/or design:

....

....

....

Specific evidence to support this:

....

....

....

....

....

Next steps in learning:

1. ....

....

....

2. ....

....

Date of nomination: ....

Name of teacher making nomination: ....

Date to review progress/review nomination: ....

Signature of head of department: ....

Peer nomination

This can be considered quite controversial but one particular case study cites a school where the head of art had been off work with a long-term illness. The able pupils coordinator for the school wanted to draw up her final cohort list and was waiting for the art nominations. She decided to ask the pupils in each art lesson who in their class had particular artistic abilities. The pupils identified a handful of peers, based mainly on things they knew those named pupils did outside school or on specific activities the coordinator had not thought about. The small number of names turned out to be an accurate selection of able pupils, confirmed by the head of art on her return to school as surprisingly well-informed. Her only changes were one or two additions whom she felt showed exceptional potential!

Parental nomination

Perhaps all parents think their child is brilliant at everything he/she does! But in most cases, parents will give the school or department insight into their child's interests, passions and specialist abilities outside school that staff may not have known about otherwise. If given the correct guidance, a department or school can ensure they get back specific information from parents that will assist in their identification or provision process. In Barry Teare's book *Effective Provision for Able and Talented Children* (1997), he gives an example of a letter that can be written to parents to assist in this process (see opposite).

As a parent, wouldn't it be wonderful to receive a letter like this? How proactive! Shouts of: 'Someone is really taking an interest in educating my child!!'

Obviously, this is a generic letter which may be sent to all parents/guardians by the able pupils coordinator or senior management team in a school, but equally it can easily be used as a framework when constructing a specific art and design letter to parents, where you may describe particular art and design skills such as drawing from memory or real life, constructing and making using found materials, a passion for aspects of art and design, and so on to assist parents in their replies. This will result in more informed identification of able pupils and gets over the most common comment at parents' evenings: 'He/she's brilliant at copying cartoons!' – How many times have you heard that?! Not that drawing cartoons isn't a particular skill in itself . . .

The debate about whether or not to inform parents that their child is very able still goes on in schools. The main reason for **not** informing them is that it may cause conflict between their child and others who are not identified, perhaps those who have gone through their schooling together, have achieved similar grades, their parents are friends, and so on. The school must have clear and transparent methods of identification so that if such a situation should arise (in reality this rarely happens) it can give a sound explanation to any parents who are concerned. It is a matter which individual schools must decide upon but it is felt, certainly by the DfES, that parents have a right to know. Having high ability is a special need, and we inform parents of exactly what our schools are doing for their child for all other special needs so why not this one? Parents are delighted to be informed and appreciate the school/department's efforts in providing the best and most appropriate education for their child.

Dear Parents,

ABLE AND TALENTED PUPILS

By law, schools have to draw up a register of pupils with Special Educational Needs and then to take steps in a prescribed order as outlined in the Code of Practice. This school also wishes to draw up a register of pupils who are particularly able in one or more activity or curriculum area. This ability could be in a subject area within the classroom or it could be in an activity outside the school. The register would help us to ensure that students' activities were being catered for in a variety of ways.

This letter is an invitation for you to write to me with information. Much of what you say will be already known by members of staff. Such information will not be wasted as it will help confirm views held by the school. Other information may well be additional to what we already know and will therefore be particularly useful.

We are not looking just for nominations of truly outstanding pupils. Research would indicate that perhaps in excess of 30% of the children in this school could justifiably be nominated in one area or another - especially when we consider all human talents and abilities.

There are some problems associated with this process. Many parents, not surprisingly, look very favourably upon their children and this may lead to a falsely high opinion of ability. Another factor which could inflate an estimate of ability is that parents do not have the same opportunities to compare a large number of children, unlike teachers. Despite these potential problems, I still believe it is sensible to ask your views. Parents spend more time with their children than do teachers and they see them in different circumstances. As a consequence they are sometimes aware of talents and abilities which have not been spotted elsewhere.

If you believe that your child does have a particular talent or possesses a high ability could you please write to me, naming the area(s) of ability and explain why you think this to be the case.

Yours sincerely,

Sample letter to parents

Indicators

Whether we call these pupils 'gifted', 'talented', 'able', 'highly able', 'more able' or 'very able' the real problem lies in how we recognise their ability and, especially in a subject such as art and design, avoid being too restrictive in our identification processes. For example you may find the 'exceptional performance' or Level 8 descriptors for the end of Key Stage 3 do not take into account certain aspects of the subject to allow for inclusivity. In some circumstances, high grades may be given for detailed, carefully executed work but recognition should also be given for originality and 'flair' which are equally important talents, particularly for those pupils who are not as adept with materials but are cognitively very able. Similarly, an ability to successfully transfer work from two into three dimensions takes a lot of skill and is not always a strong part of formally agreed assessment criteria. Achievement and ability are not necessarily the same.

The art and design indicators

Pupils with talent in art and design will show evidence of **exceptional** ability in:

- using artistic media to record accurately what is observed
- recalling accurately from memory when using artistic media for visual and expressive purposes
- recording observed three-dimensional forms in two dimensions, using appropriate perspective
- controlling an artistic medium and related tools and equipment. These include graphic media, paint, clay and other three-dimensional construction media. *For example, pencils: accurate tonal graduation using appropriate choice of hard and soft pencils; clay: ability to use a range of tools and processes to create a detailed ceramic model, etc.*
- the expressive use of an artistic medium such as paint or clay
- an understanding of the use/manipulation of the visual elements of art and design. *For example, ability to mix a wide range of tones from a limited range; ability to simulate a wide range of surface textures using graphic media; an innovatory approach to composition; the ability to understand confidently and engage in the process of developing an abstract design from an observed source, etc.*
- originality and exercise of the imagination in the development and interpretation of visual ideas
- confident engagement in the process of visual enquiry, and in selecting from a range of stimuli and starting points to incorporate elements imaginatively in their finished work
- critical engagement with the work of artists and designers, which may positively influence their own creative endeavours

(Adapted from the 'Creative Generation' website: www.creativegeneration.co.uk)

Obviously, these are broad indicators and it is for the teacher to decide on the individual ability of the pupil in comparison to others of the same age. They will also help in allowing the teacher to identify potential high ability and can act as prompts to provide activities in their units of work that allow for these indicators to be seen and assessed.

National Curriculum level descriptors may also help in the identification process. The DfES has asked some LEAs recently to report on their Level 7s and above as a means of formally recording the achievement of our more able pupils. It would be a worthwhile exercise to assess pupil work in light of these descriptors at various stages throughout Key Stage 3 rather than just at the end. The National Curriculum says that at the end of Key Stage 3, Level 7 pupils in art and design will:

- explore ideas and assess visual and other information, analysing codes and conventions used in different genres, styles and traditions

- select, organise and present information in visual and other ways, taking account of purpose and audience

- extend their understanding of materials and processes and interpret visual and tactile qualities

- show increasing independence in the way in which they develop ideas and meanings and realise their intentions

- analyse and comment on the context of their own and others' work

- explain how their own ideas, experiences and values affect their views and practice.

If we look at the Level 8 descriptors, notice that the difference between the two seems to be that Level 8 involves the pupil making much more use of *higher order thinking skills* (Bloom's taxonomy), highlighted below in italics, and one could argue that this may be the true 'more able' level as for many years, these particular thinking skills have been used to challenge and stretch pupils. The National Curriculum says that Level 8 pupils will:

- explore ideas and *evaluate* relevant visual and other information, *analysing* how codes and conventions are used to present ideas, beliefs and values in different genres, styles and traditions

- *research*, document and present in visual and other ways appropriate to their purpose and audience

- *exploit the potential* of materials and processes to develop ideas and meanings, realise their intentions and *sustain their investigations*

- *evaluate* the contexts of their own and others' work, *articulating* similarities and differences in their views and practice

- *further develop* their ideas and their work in light of insights gained from others.

The 'exceptional performance' descriptors highlight a pupil who has an immense passion for art combined with the artistic and verbal skills to compliment and represent that passion. Again, higher order thinking skill usage is key. Pupils:

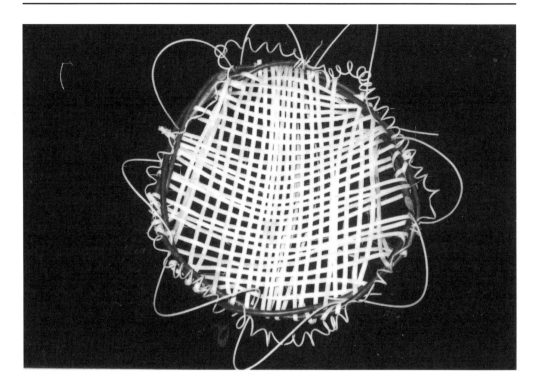

- explore ideas, *critically evaluate* relevant visual and other information and *make connections* between representations in different genres, styles and traditions

- *initiate research*, and document and interpret information in visual and other ways appropriate to their purpose and audience

- *exploit* the characteristics of materials and processes to develop ideas and meanings and realise their intentions

- *extend their ideas* and sustain their investigations by responding to new possibilities and meanings

- identify why ideas and meanings in others' work are subject to different interpretations, using their understanding to extend their thinking and practical work

- communicate their own ideas, insights and views.

> How well a school identifies its more able pupils will largely depend on the range of learning opportunities that it offers . . . young people can only demonstrate their abilities if they are given the opportunity to do so. The process of auditing existing provision is likely to aid in their identification by raising awareness and capacity of the institution as a whole to recognise the full range of skills and aptitudes. Ofsted evaluations suggest that if under-identification is to be avoided, a specific approach for each subject area needs to be fully developed.
>
> (Extract from QCA 'Guidance on Teaching the Gifted and Talented', on the QCA website www.qca.org.uk)

Multiple intelligences, preferred learning styles and Bloom's taxonomy

Once identified as being strong in one or more particular 'intelligences' and favouring a particular learning style, we should use this knowledge to understand how we learn best at any given moment. We must recognise that it is in our own interests to learn in a variety of ways and that our learning style may change as we get older or more experienced in a particular field. By planning projects or units of work that address this variety of styles, teachers can ensure that every child's individual strengths are catered for but also that they are being given plenty of opportunities to learn in different ways. Higher levels of challenge could be built into individual guidance that is given to more able pupils within their preferred learning style. As teachers, we probably teach to our own preferred styles of learning and need to ensure that we come out of our 'comfort zone' in the best interests of our pupils to deliver our lessons using a range of strategies and techniques. But as art teachers, we are used to doing this – 2D, 3D, pencil, textiles, observing, annotating, discussing, evaluating, etc.

> I want my children to understand the world, but not just because the world is fascinating and the human mind is curious. I want them to understand it so that they will be positioned to make it a better place. Knowledge is not the same as morality, but we need to understand if we are to avoid past mistakes and move in productive directions. An important part of that understanding is knowing who we are and what we can do . . . Ultimately, we must synthesize our understandings for ourselves.
>
> (Howard Gardner, 1999)

The theory of multiple intelligences has again been brought to the fore in current educational developments through the 'Gifted and Talented Initiative' in the UK. It was developed in 1983 by Dr Howard Gardner, Professor of Education at Harvard University in the United States and written about in his book *Frames of Mind* (1983). The theory suggests that the traditional notion of intelligence, based on IQ testing, is far too limited. Instead, Gardner proposes eight different intelligences to account for a broader range of human potential in children and adults. These intelligences are:

- **linguistic intelligence** (strong in reading, writing, telling stories, memorising dates, thinking in words)

- **logical–mathematical intelligence** (strong in maths, reasoning, logic, problem-solving, patterns)

- **spatial intelligence** (strong in reading, maps, charts, drawing, mazes, puzzles, imaging things, visualisation)

- **bodily–kinaesthetic intelligence** (strong in sport, dancing, acting, crafts, using tools)

- **musical intelligence** (strong in singing, picking up sounds, remembering melodies, rhythms)

- **interpersonal intelligence** (strong in understanding people, leading, organising, communicating, resolving conflicts, selling)

- **intrapersonal intelligence** (strong in understanding self, recognising strengths and weaknesses, setting goals)

- **naturalist intelligence** (strong in understanding nature, making distinctions, identifying flora and fauna).

Linguistic intelligence involves sensitivity to spoken and written language, the ability to learn languages and the capacity to use language to accomplish certain goals. This intelligence includes the ability to use language effectively to express oneself rhetorically or poetically, and language as a means to remember information. Writers, poets, lawyers and speakers are among those that Howard Gardner sees as having high linguistic intelligence.

- Learns best through reading, hearing and seeing words, speaking, writing, discussing and debating

Logical–mathematical intelligence consists of the capacity to analyse problems logically, carry out mathematical operations and investigate issues scientifically. In Howard Gardner's words, it entails the ability to detect patterns, reason deductively and think logically. This intelligence is most often associated with scientific and mathematical thinking.

- Learns best through working with patterns and relationships, classifying, categorising, working with the abstract

Spatial intelligence involves the potential to recognise and use the patterns of wide space and more confined areas.

- Learns best through working with pictures and colours, visualising, drawing

Bodily–kinaesthetic intelligence entails the potential of using one's whole body or parts of the body to solve problems. It is the ability to use mental abilities to coordinate bodily movements. Howard Gardner sees mental and physical activity as related.

- Learns best through touching, moving, processing knowledge through bodily sensations

Musical intelligence involves skill in the performance, composition and appreciation of musical patterns. It encompasses the capacity to recognise and compose musical pitches, tones and rhythms. According to Howard Gardner, musical intelligence runs in an almost structural parallel to linguistic intelligence.

- Learns best through rhythm, melody, singing, listening to music and melodies and sound in general

Interpersonal intelligence is concerned with the capacity to understand the intentions, motivations and desires of other people. It allows people to work effectively with others. Educators, salespeople, religious and political leaders and counsellors all need a well-developed interpersonal intelligence.

- Learns best through sharing, comparing, relating, interviewing, cooperating

Intrapersonal intelligence entails the capacity to understand oneself, to appreciate one's feelings, fears and motivations. In Howard Gardner's view it involves having an effective working model of ourselves, and to be able to use such information to regulate our lives.

- Learns best through working alone, doing self-paced projects, having space, reflecting

Naturalist intelligence involves the full range of knowing that occurs in and through our encounters with the natural world including our recognition, appreciation and understanding of the natural environment. It involves such capacities as species discernment, communion with the natural world and its phenomena, and the ability to recognise and classify various flora and fauna.

- Learns best through working in nature, exploring things, learning about plants and natural events

Gardner says that our schools and culture focus most of their attention on linguistic and logical–mathematical intelligence. We hold in high esteem the highly articulate or logical people of our culture. However, he feels that we should also place equal attention on individuals who show gifts in the other intelligences: the artists, architects, musicians, naturalists, designers, dancers, therapists, entrepreneurs and others who enrich the world in which we live. In the past, many children who had these gifts did not receive much reinforcement for them in school. Many of them, in fact, ended up being labelled, often as simply 'underachievers', when their unique ways of thinking and learning were not addressed by a heavily linguistic or logical–mathematical classroom.

The theory of multiple intelligences proposes a major transformation in the way our schools are run. It suggests that teachers of all subject areas be trained to present their lessons in a wide variety of ways using music, cooperative learning, art activities, role play, multimedia, field trips, inner reflection and much more. The good news is that the theory of multiple intelligences has grabbed the attention of many educators around the country, and some schools are starting to use its philosophy to redesign the way they educate children. The even better news is that good art teachers, through the very nature of the subject, have always catered for multiple intelligences by offering a range of projects and activities that necessitate pupils using a wide variety of skills. The bad news is that there is still a long way to go before all schools get rid of teacher-talk and boring worksheets! As all teaching and non-teaching staff in schools become more informed on what multiple intelligences are, children will have the opportunity to learn in ways that are most beneficial to them . . . and not the educators.

Preferred learning styles

You may have noticed that when you try to learn something new that you perhaps prefer to learn by listening to someone talk to you about the information. Some people prefer to read about a concept to learn it; others need to see a demonstration of the concept. Learning style theory proposes that different people learn in different ways and that it is good to know what your own preferred learning style is. As previously mentioned, we probably also teach to our preferred learning style for a majority of the time so it is worth spending some time revisiting our lesson planning to make sure that we deliver our lessons using a variety of methods and that our students are learning using a variety of methods or approaches over the course of a unit of work.

There are three main learning styles: visual, auditory and kinaesthetic, often referred to as 'VAK'. If you carry out an internet search on 'learning styles' you will find numerous 'tests' to help you identify yours. You may be kinaesthetic or visual, you may be a combination of two or you may even find that your learning is split across all three styles, making you a learner who would gain something from all teaching approaches without much difficulty! As we get older, we learn how to learn in different ways in order to make the most of anything we are presented with, but children usually take longer to learn how to adapt. As with multiple intelligences, identifying your preferred learning style only tells you how you learn best at this moment in time. You may learn best in a different way next year so again, we must be wary of 'labelling' ourselves as a visual, auditory or kinaesthetic learner.

Visual learners:

- take numerous detailed notes
- tend to sit in the front
- are usually neat and clean
- often close their eyes to visualise or remember something
- find something to watch if they are bored
- like to see what they are learning
- benefit from illustrations and presentations that use colour
- are attracted to written or spoken language rich in imagery
- prefer stimuli to be isolated from auditory and kinaesthetic distraction
- find passive surroundings ideal.

Auditory learners:

- sit where they can hear but need not pay attention to what is happening in front
- may not coordinate colours or clothes, but can explain why they are wearing them
- hum or talk to themselves or others when bored
- acquire knowledge by reading aloud
- remember by verbalising lessons to themselves (if they do not, they have difficulty reading maps or diagrams or handling conceptual assignments like mathematics).

Kinaesthetic learners:

- need to be active and take frequent breaks
- speak with their hands and with gestures
- remember what was done, but have difficulty recalling what was said or seen
- find reasons to tinker or move when bored
- rely on what they can directly experience or perform
- find that activities such as cooking, construction, engineering and art help them perceive and learn
- enjoy field trips and tasks that involve manipulating materials
- sit near the door or somewhere else where they can easily get up and move around
- are uncomfortable in classrooms where they lack opportunities for hands-on experience
- communicate by touching and appreciate physically expressed encouragement, such as a pat on the back.

Of course, these are general descriptions and not all bullet points apply to that particular style of learner. The good thing to remember about art and design is that in almost every lesson, pupils will experience each style because the subject demands it. For example, pupils are always allowed to get up out of their seats to get something – a pencil, glue, etc. In fact, they are encouraged to, especially the more able pupil who is working more independently and extending their own practice in lesson time. For them, the art teacher does not need to dictate or steer the pupil every step of the way. For kinaesthetic learners, this movement is important but you can see how it may get them into trouble in other subjects! 'Chalk and talk' teaching does not cater for these children and so often many of them end up in lower sets or underachieving. How many times have we assumed that daydreamers are not listening or thinking about what we have been discussing in class? Do they really need to *look* at the teacher to listen? How many visual learners are identified as highly able in art purely because they are neat and tidy?

Pupils do not need to take 'tests' to find out their preferred learning style unless the teacher wishes them to for a bit of fun. In practice, it is sometimes hard for them to understand that there is not a right or wrong way of doing things! As long as teacher planning and delivery caters for each style within a unit of work, all children will benefit by learning how to learn in different ways.

Bloom's taxonomy

In 1956, Benjamin Bloom headed a group of educational psychologists who developed a classification of levels of intellectual behaviour important in learning. Bloom found that over 95 per cent of the test questions students encounter require them to think only at the lowest possible level . . . the recall of information. Bloom's taxonomy is a way to classify instructional activities or questions as they progress in difficulty. The lower levels require less in the way of thinking skills and as we move up the hierarchy, the activities require higher level thinking skills. It is the inclusion of these higher order thinking skills (HOTS) in lesson planning that allows more able pupils in art and design to be stretched and to do something further with their prior learning and new knowledge. This, quite simply, is differentiation.

Bloom's taxonomy – thinking skills	
EVALUATION	Comparing, discriminating, prioritising, verifying, assessing, recommending . . .
SYNTHESIS	Relating, generalising, combining, creating, predicting, concluding . . .
ANALYSIS	Recognising patterns, components, hidden meanings . . .
APPLICATION	Using knowledge, method, concepts, solving problems . . .
COMPREHENSION	Understanding, interpreting, comparing, contrasting, ordering . . .
KNOWLEDGE	Facts, figures, information, observation, recall . . .

The higher order thinking skills – analysis, synthesis and evaluation – are those most used with able pupils. Look back at the Level 8 descriptors for the end of

Key Stage 3 in the National Curriculum (page 34), where the emphasis lies on these particular skills.

The QCA website 'Gifted and talented guidance for art and design' suggests the teacher promotes creative thinking alongside HOTS:

> By using thinking skills, pupils can focus on knowing *how*, as well as knowing *what*, to learn. Art and design includes activities that enable pupils to reflect on their own thinking processes and clarify and reflect on problem-solving strategies. These activities include:
>
> ● teacher reflection on, and modelling of, thinking skills
>
> ● problem solving in pairs
>
> ● cooperative learning
>
> ● group discussions.
>
> Exploring and developing ideas in art and design offers opportunities for developing creative thinking, enquiry, information processing, reasoning and evaluation.
>
> (From the QCA National Curriculum website
> www.nc.uk.net/gt/art/teaching_thinkingskills.htm)

Creative thinking skills enable pupils to generate and extend ideas, to suggest hypotheses, to apply imagination and to look for innovative outcomes.

Pupils are required to generate imaginative ideas for the production of their work and then apply those ideas to facilitate the development of new insights or ways of understanding. In art and design lessons, teachers should plan for pupils to:

● **generate and extend ideas** – for example, when generating a wider range of information, they locate and collect relevant ideas as part of a class collective sketchbook based on the project theme, or employ the 'If . . . then' technique during discussions, such as 'If Gauguin had not travelled to the South Sea Islands, then . . .'

● **suggest hypotheses** – for example, when they make conjectures about the iconography used in paintings of the Middle Ages or about the political influences of Eastern European art

● **apply imagination** – for example, when they explore the imaginative use of materials through artists such as Chris Ofili (elephant dung), Damian Hurst (formaldehyde) or Tony Cragg (collected rubbish), or employ the imaginative use of specialist art forms such as photography in exploring the representation of images

● **look for alternative outcomes** – for example, when they explore unusual themes or starting points, such as 'object transformation' through the concepts advocated by Surrealists like Meret Oppenheim (fur-covered cup, saucer and spoon) or explore the concepts of scale and proportion through the ideas of Pop Artists such as Claes Oldenburg.

Enquiry skills enable pupils to ask relevant questions, to pose and define problems, to plan what to do and ways to research, to predict outcomes and anticipate consequences, and to test conclusions and improve ideas.

Information-processing skills enable pupils to locate and collect relevant information, to sort, clarify, sequence, compare and contrast, and to analyse the relationship of parts to the whole.

Reasoning skills enable pupils to support opinions and actions, to draw references and make deductions, to use precise language to explain thoughts, and to make judgements and decisions informed by reasons and/or evidence.

Evaluation skills enable pupils to evaluate information, to judge the value of what they read, hear and do, to develop criteria for judging the value of their own and others' work or ideas, and to have confidence in their judgements. Teachers should plan for pupils to:

- **evaluate information** – for example, when they use a SWOT (strengths, weaknesses, opportunities, threats) analysis to determine their impressions regarding the effectiveness of the composition of paintings, such as those by the Fauvist painters

- **judge the value of what they read, hear and do** – for example, when they evaluate the quality of sketchbook work at each stage in the development of a piece of design work, or evaluate the thoughts and emotions of an artist through the study of their recorded letters or diaries

- **develop criteria for judging the value of their own and others' work and ideas** – for example, when they employ peer assessment, where pupils exchange their sketchbook work to identify what is good and not so good in others' work and what they find interesting and why

- **have confidence in their judgements** – for example, when they decide which media to employ (and when) in a mixed media monochrome drawing based on the sketches and experiments they conducted as part of their preliminary studies.

Through fully utilising these approaches, art teachers should ensure that able pupils are given the opportunity to explore the subject in more depth and breadth than others, as and when required, in order to keep them motivated and enjoying their learning. The quality of their work should be monitored closely and teachers' input, as with all other pupils, should move them on towards more challenging goals. The following extract is taken from the Key Stage 3 National Strategy materials for teaching gifted and talented pupils in art and design.

The principle: MAKE LEARNING ACTIVE

Defining features for able pupils:

- Teaching uses a wide range of stimuli to take account of the preferred learning styles of able pupils.
- Teaching uses questioning strategies to support higher order thinking.
- The classroom environment encourages pupils to use generic, transferable thinking skills activities.

In particular, in art and design:

- Teaching provides a range of opportunities to allow able pupils to exploit the characteristics of materials and processes in the development of personal ideas, explore alternatives and respond to new possibilities and meanings.

Examples

Colour and space in images of the landscape: Turner's landscape paintings are compared with those of the fauves in a project looking at the use of colour to evoke space in pictorial representations of the landscape. Able pupils select and use appropriate options from a range of media, to explore the expressive possibilities presented by their developing understanding of how colour relates to composition.

'Mr & Mrs Beckham': In this project, pupils explore ideas and feelings about their own culture. They analyse paintings in order to learn how visual qualities can be manipulated to evoke strong reactions and to represent ideas, beliefs and values. They make connections between eighteenth- and nineteenth-century paintings and contemporary visual culture. For example Holbein's 'The Ambassadors', Gainsborough's 'Mr & Mrs Andrews', Frida Kahlo's 'Me and my sister', and Andrew Wyeth's 'Farmer and his wife'. Able pupils will synthesise their understanding of the key elements of contemporary culture in response to the project title 'Mr & Mrs Beckham'.

Classroom provision

- Planning in the art department
- Differentiation
- Homework

Planning in the art department

Effective planning in the art department takes account of the different abilities and interests of each pupil allowing them to progress and demonstrate their achievements, whilst making for effective learning and an effective learning environment. A balanced programme of study is one which develops skills in painting, drawing, collage, 3D work, printing and textiles and develops an understanding of colour, line, texture, pattern, shape, form and space. Progression statements in the skills and elements of each project are important when providing for the more able and work should be built upon over a period of time, rather than a series of 'one-off' lessons.

It is very important, when planning provision for more able students, to consider the following:

- your department's capacity (staffing, materials, resources, access to ICT) to provide challenge for all pupils

- breadth, depth and pace of art and design provision to allow effective identification, as well as successful learning

- the ability to tie together provision in-class, out-of-class and off-site

- study support (out-of-school-hours learning) and independent learning more generally

- grouping in the classroom.

Teachers should also be aware of specific planning that takes into account provision for pupils who may have a potential barrier to learning but may still be highly able in art and design such as those:

- who do not like being identified as 'more able' or 'talented' in art due to peer or parental pressure. You will be able to cite examples of students in some of your classes who hate being given any form of public praise, for example. Planning may have brief annotations to remind you of ways of working with these particular pupils which encourage and support them, eventually allowing them to speak out confidently thus creating a safe classroom environment for all pupils that values differences.

- who may have English as an additional language. You may need to provide extra support in the classroom as well as different tasks linked to your expected outcomes otherwise EAL students can feel alienated from certain aspects of the subject.

- who have additional needs in some areas of learning that require support. Teachers should allow them to highlight those aspects of the subject for which they show promise or particular strengths, such as three-dimensional work or use of colour and texture.

- who have specific religious beliefs. Teachers may need to adapt units to offer alternatives to these pupils in ways that ensure the core learning is not affected.

The particular able pupils listed above require a suitable curriculum where their needs are identified and provided for. Art teachers should work closely with special needs staff in the school to ensure that this is achieved.

In designing an art and design course the following aims are an integral part of the planning, bearing in mind that the expectations of process and outcome are commensurate with the pupil's level of development and ability.

Aims are:

- to develop an understanding, appreciation and enjoyment of art and design, where possible, in historical, functional and aesthetic terms

- to develop a sense of enquiry about visual and tactile experiences

- to enable pupils to realise their creative intentions, through the development of technical competence and manipulative skills

- to be aware of the social and cultural context within which a pupil lives and works

- to provide opportunities for personal and imaginative enquiry – it is essential that able pupils are given many opportunities for creative expression

- to observe, record, evaluate and order information

- to encourage pupils to be self-critical and self-motivated and to develop the ability to solve problems

- to help pupils acquire a subject-specific language

- to encourage experimentation and help develop a means of personal expression

- to have fun and enjoyment and feel stimulated by the sense of achievement in the creative process.

An essential element in art and design teaching is a degree of 'uncertainty', a chance for pupils to discover the potential of materials and processes within a 'safe' and structured environment. Art and design education should provide practical learning experiences that are accessible to pupils of all abilities. Using appropriate and differentiated work is about making tasks accessible to the whole range of pupils within a class or teaching group. In the art department a variety of differentiation methods are used rather than a reliance on one or two. This means that it is the matching of the differentiation to the pupil's needs that makes a difference not just the use of different levels and ways of working. For this reason, multi-sensory approaches are vital in the art classroom. Many skills and elements will inevitably be repeated, for example the skill of drawing, the elements of line and colour and so on and in a more able pupil's IEP (if you decide to use one) you may wish to stress progression in the development of skills and the understanding of the formal elements of art and design, especially at Key Stage 3.

It is also important to include in your planning the creation or upkeep of displays of examples of best practice and to show pupils' work and subject-specific language. This aspect is often overlooked and children will be very keen to let you know if something has been on the walls all year or longer! Art departments often run short after-school or INSET day sessions to 'train' classroom or teaching assistants or technicians (if you're lucky enough to have one!) in how to create a 'good' display. Assistants have found this is really useful and, by ensuring displays are constantly kept looking fresh or by changing them completely at certain times of the academic year, can help the classroom teacher no end. These displays may be on a planned theme for the term or may highlight best practice using specific techniques or materials. To grab interest around the school and to literally bring art outside of the classroom, it may be appropriate to display an artefact or painting, weekly or monthly and refer to this as 'Painting of the Month' for example. Simple display is often the key to success. It is important to show the process to be exhibited alongside the finished piece – photographs of pupils working, the plan of work, artefacts that extend the work and appropriate and clearly written statements. Able pupils, just as much as any other pupil, need something to 'aspire' to from time to time, or indeed, to challenge them to produce something different or more 'in-depth'.

Planning models

Extension and enrichment

The teacher or head of department may employ various planning models and it is up to the individual to decide which works best for them – after all, it takes up most of our time as a teacher and is at the heart of excellence in learning and teaching. The most common form of planning for more able pupils is by having a core unit of work which is used for pupils of all abilities, with **enrichment** and in particular, **extension** work built in.

Enrichment relates to breadth of study and experience. It involves offering learners a wide variety of opportunities, both within and outside the curriculum, and exposing them to experiences not usually encountered as part of the standard curriculum. If it relies on too many unplanned or bolt-on extracurricular activities, it can lead to eclectic provision. Enrichment delivered through breadth around a subject area should be linked closely with extension work through depth of learning or to plans for acceleration or faster pace of study, for example entering pupils for GCSE Art in Year 9.

Extension involves students following the standard curriculum but developing a deeper understanding through encountering more complex resources and materials, tackling more challenging questions and tasks, demonstrating higher levels of thinking, and presenting increasingly sophisticated responses.

Extension is not about giving able students more work to do than everyone else, for example, extra homework; it should not be about giving them more of the same, nor should it be about accelerating them through the content of the unit of work. It heavily relies upon teachers having a sound understanding of what a high-level response to a particular aspect of art and design may be or look like; teachers need to know this so that they can differentiate accurately in terms of expectation and performance. Teachers should also ask questions and probe the thinking of pupils without necessarily having the answer themselves or without expecting there to be a 'right' answer as there often is not in art and design – this takes the confidence of a teacher who doesn't need to come across as the 'font of all knowledge' all the time! This makes for more independent learners who have confidence in their own ability.

The development of pupils' thinking skills plays an important part in this, and exploring ideas is a key element. Of course, in providing these particular opportunities, teachers can be fully equipped for any students who were not originally identified as more able and may show their true colours by having this type of work available to them too – remember, we are always talking about **inclusive** provision rather then **exclusive**.

QCA give examples of activities that could be used to **extend** and **enrich** pupils' art and design work, which are shown below. They are based on the QCA/DfES schemes of work for art and design.

Key Stage 3, Year 9: Environmental Design

Unit 9c: Personal places, public spaces – this unit focuses on environmental design

(Extension task) Ask talented pupils to analyse the ideas, methods and approaches of a local environmental artist or designer (for example, an architect, town planner, sculptor or landscape artist of the past or present) and make connections with their own work.

(Enrichment task) Encourage the pupils to experiment with a range of three-dimensional materials and processes and develop alternative forms and sequences of forms. Where possible, explore the possibilities for casting or transforming their designs into more permanent materials.

(Enrichment task) Organise an opportunity for the pupils to present their own designs, photographs and models to an outside audience (for example, local businesses or town planners) and get critical feedback on their proposals for a mural, sculpture or three-dimensional functional form, including its suggested siting.

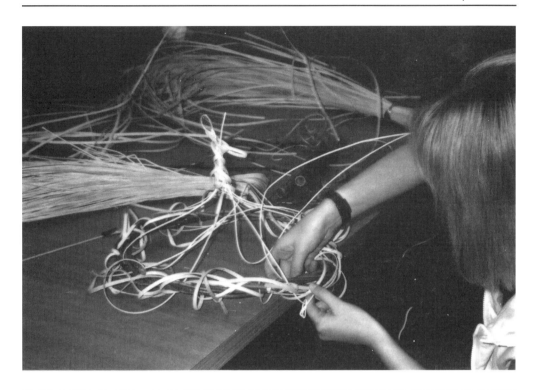

Key Stage 4, Year 11: Citizenship

Personal or group project relating to citizenship

(Extension AND Enrichment tasks)

Ask talented pupils to research a spiritual or cultural issue by analysing information from different sources, including first-hand contact with local artists and craftspeople. Ask them to design a mural to be located in the community and to work collaboratively to make this.

Make arrangements for them to negotiate with community leaders to site the mural in order to communicate different perspectives and experiences in relation to the issue.

End of unit expectations in art and design

This planning model uses specific wording to introduce a description of what pupils will have learned by the time they reach the end of a unit of work. It is usually a good idea to start at the end so that teacher planning focuses entirely on what you want your students to learn and then activities can be considered in relation to the intended outcomes. The wording for each paragraph is as follows:

At the end of this unit

'Most pupils will . . .' – this relates to the core of the unit that most of the group or class will be expected to achieve by a certain time. This section should ensure coverage of the formal elements of art and design, incorporate some thinking skills and allow for the development of ideas. Pupils should realise their intentions following a refining and adapting of ideas.

'Some pupils will not have made so much progress and will . . .' – this paragraph will discuss what progress a smaller number of pupils can be expected to achieve if they have additional needs, have been absent or generally struggle with some aspects of the subject, requiring further support. They will not, therefore, cover as many areas as described above. In planning, teachers should stipulate exactly what it is essential to cover with these pupils in order to ensure progression, even if limited.

'Some pupils will have progressed further and will . . .' – this is the section aimed at more able pupils and may incorporate the extension and enrichment provision as discussed previously. The use of higher order thinking skills can be highlighted here to build upon pupils' learning through the core of the unit.

The following unit of work has been compiled to cover Key Stage 3 or 4 depending upon the ability of the group of pupils in the school. It uses the above planning model and also incorporates the use of higher order thinking skills (Bloom's taxonomy) for the more able student and visual, auditory and kinaesthetic learning styles. It can be adapted to suit a range of abilities and all resources can be obtained easily via the internet or publications listed at the end of the unit.

See Appendix 4.1 and the accompanying CD for:

- what the unit covers and aims and objectives

- pupil activity sheets

- teacher checklist for evaluating progress

- list of resource material

- background information sheet

Adaptable art, craft and design Key Stage 3/4 unit of work – 'IDENTITY'

At the end of this unit

Most pupils will:

analyse and comment on ideas surrounding identity or self-image and approaches to representing an image of self through shape, form and space; compare the approach of Cindy Sherman and their own work; record and explore ideas through role play and digital photography, developing and extending their skills; combining and manipulating collage and three-dimensional techniques to make a mask, exploring colour, pattern, form and shape; reflect on, adapt and refine their work to realise their own ideas and intentions.

Some pupils will not have made so much progress and will:

comment on similarities and differences between Cindy Sherman's work and their own; represent themselves through observational drawing and digital photography; experiment with collage and mask-making techniques to move from two-dimensional to three-dimensional work; adapt and improve their work.

*(more able) Some pupils will have progressed further and will:

critically assess Cindy Sherman's and others' ideas, methods and approaches and analyse their codes and conventions (e.g. Edward Hopper, Sherrie Levine); experiment with and select ideas, methods and approaches to use in their own work and interpret shape, form and space in two and three-dimensional representation (observational work, digital photography, mask-making); explain how their understanding of 'identity', Sherman's and others' work has influenced their practice, making links with Postmodernist theory.

Nottingham Excellence in Cities have put together a 'gifted and talented' lesson plan checklist in their 'monitoring and assessment' guidance which art teachers may find useful (see overleaf). Teachers place a tick and their initials next to each of the key points.

The 'must, should, could' model

This model stems from National Curriculum guidance and is a short-term method of planning that allows teachers to cover all abilities within their lessons. It is very similar to the end of unit descriptors as described above, in that 'must' means that all pupils **must** achieve specific or core outcomes by a certain time; 'should' means that a majority of pupils **should** achieve further outcomes; and 'could' means that the more able pupils **could** also achieve even further or different outcomes relating to the core or theme by a certain time. The pro forma on page 55 could be used by teachers when planning (an amendable copy can be found on the accompanying CD).

Art department gifted and talented lesson plan checklist

Able pupils coordinator for art and design: ....

Date: ....

FOCUS	KEY POINTS	TEACHER	TEACHER	TEACHER	TEACHER
Objectives	Are learning objectives set for more able pupils?				
Activities	Do activities relate to developing higher order thinking skills?				
Use of assessment	Is assessment used to show pupils what they need to do to reach the highest levels?				
Resources	Are resources challenging and inspiring?				
Home learning	Is home learning challenging, interesting and differentiated?				

Mind mapping

The use of mind maps when planning work, either by pupils (as a classroom activity or as homework) or teachers (as shown here – a planning method), allows the learner to use their visual, auditory and kinaesthetic (V, A or K) learning styles all at the same time. There are five basic steps to mind mapping and these are:

1. The teacher puts all his/her thoughts and prior knowledge around a topic area down on paper (V and K). For example, 'Natural Forms' as a title with areas

Short-term planning sheet using the 'must, should, could' model

Project title or theme: . . . .   Year or group: . . . .

	MUST Defining the task	SHOULD Exploring the task	COULD Developing the task
Starting points			
Learning outcomes or concepts			
Unit of study			
Activities			
Assessment opportunities			
Resources/ideas for teachers			

relating to this also listed such as feathers, shells, plants, trees, leaves and twigs, insect body parts, etc.

2. The related areas are then grouped together as themes within a theme. These could be colour coded to allow further clarity when reading (V and K).

3. The next step requires the teacher to add further information once the topic has been researched in more detail. So, for example, from the words 'leaves and twigs' may come 'Andy Goldsworthy' or 'shades of green, brown, blue and red'. From the word 'shells' may come 'Georgia O'Keefe' or the words 'shiny, opalescent, pastel', etc. This is a refining process that makes the information more relevant to the central theme and is actually building up a unit of work (V and K).

4. The information should then be plotted visually on a mind map (as shown below) to give a structure to thought processes. Colours can be added to the different 'branches' coming from the centre, as can images that are drawn or collaged on to assist in the recall process but also to make the mind map look more interesting! (V and K)

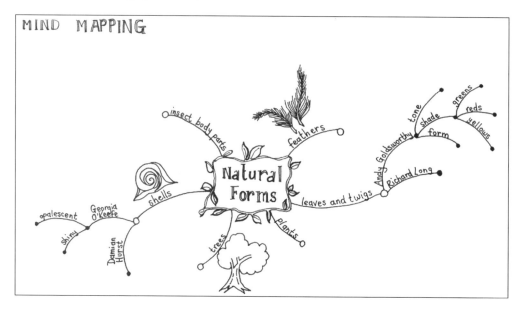

5. The final step is to explain and talk through the mind map with another person. This could be done by all members of the art department at a departmental meeting, for example in the summer term as everyone is planning for the year ahead. As you explain to your partner, you should use your finger to trace over the map, following the paths or branches to give clarification. They can ask you questions about the topic as you go (V, A and K).

Differentiation

Classroom provision for the more able pupil is merely a form of differentiation. There are many different types of differentiation and it is time well spent in understanding what these are and applying them in an art and design context in order to benefit all pupils. Through differentiation in the curriculum teachers are able to plan so that not everyone does the same thing – tasks are varied to provide for individual needs (the National Curriculum increases the scope for teachers to provide able pupils with appropriately challenging materials, which may be selected, if necessary, from later key stages). The most common forms of differentiation, which allow students to work at their own level, are shown here and are available on the PowerPoint presentation on the accompanying CD. The presentation may be used for whole-staff INSET in a school or just within the art department to consider how these methods may apply to art and design. The methods are as follows:

Types of differentiation

- by outcome
- by resource
- by task
- by dialogue
- by support
- by pace
- by content
- by independence or responsibility.

By outcome

- same materials/tasks for all students
- open-ended tasks essential for this
- individuals answer/respond at their own level of ability
- teacher to set up planning strategies for the task.

By resource

- more advanced material/tasks, perhaps on same theme as all students
- materials/tasks are more detailed and require greater depth of understanding/higher skill level
- wide variety of resources needed
- teacher to set up planning strategies for the task.

By task

- variety of tasks provided by teacher that cover main content area
- more able students can start further along and do not need same starting point
- fewer 'steps' to be incorporated into planning
- more damage done by not catering to individual needs than social aspect of giving different tasks.

By dialogue

- emphasis on the role of the teacher, talking to and with students
- vocabulary and complexity of language used needs to vary. It should be at a more sophisticated level for the able student

- teacher should prompt and encourage students with comments suitable to the ability of the student and degree of progress being made.

By support

- links with dialogue
- differentiate the amount and degree of help provided. More able may require an independent learning package
- this support can be provided by teachers, classroom assistants, learning mentors, etc.
- the nature of the support should vary.

By pace

- many able students can sustain a quicker programme and become frustrated if pace is not strong enough
- simple tasks can be made more difficult if they need to be achieved in a limited time
- differentiate lesson plans in terms of how much and how quickly tasks are to be completed.

By content

- teachers can incorporate different 'dimensions' to classroom or out-of-hours activities
- these do not have to be National Curriculum based.

By independence or responsibility

- teachers can incorporate sections of lessons or out-of-hours activities that are planned by the student
- teachers can ensure that progress is made even though the student has taken responsibility for their own learning.

Examples of differentiation for able pupils in art and design

By outcome

For example – Year 10: pupils are asked to bring in an old shoe, boot or trainer. Following research and discussions on the work of an artist or designer, they must decorate the piece of footwear so that it represents that artist or designer's style of working, methods of working or thinking/philosophy behind their working. The teacher should have a wide assortment of materials available for all students to select from such as fabric, coloured paper, threads, tools such as craft knives (health and safety rules apply), thin wire and so on. The emphasis of this part of the unit of work may be to allow pupils to work on different surfaces and to build their confidence away from a flat, two-dimensional way of working. Less able pupils will need more guidance and support from the teacher as to the best way to approach the task, whereas the more able pupil should have developed their own ideas during planning stages in their sketchbook, small group or class discussions that utilise higher order thinking and through one-to-one dialogue with the teacher. They may wish to create their own materials to use on the piece of footwear such as digital images on paper or transferred onto fabric, collages of the artist or designer's work or small objects they have brought in or found. They may wish to cut away part of the shoe, make their own shoe or not even to use a shoe at all but another item of adornment that may be more 'in keeping' with the artist or designer they have researched. The task is open-ended and the teacher has allowed 'space' for artistic skills and talents to be developed and realised by the end of a set amount of time.

By resource

For example – Year 7: the teacher sets up a still life using a selection of 'tropical' plants and flowers with artefacts of African origin. It is lit using small spotlights that uplight and cast shadows on a background of fabric or coloured paper. The more able pupil may be asked by the teacher to concentrate particularly upon the way the light hits the objects and casts shadow, thus ensuring they use the formal elements of tone and form, possibly introducing distortion and chiaroscuro and new materials/techniques such as oil pastels or charcoal which the pupil may not have used in primary school. The more able pupil's work will differ in outcome from others in the group as his/her skills have been extended through exploration, experimentation and teacher support.

By task

For example – Year 8: pupils are given different tasks within the same theme of the unit, depending on their ability in art and design. Pupils may be asked by the teacher to research a craftsperson/designer such as René Lalique for homework to complement work being done in class on body adornment. Each 'tier' of homework may be numbered or printed out on a different colour of paper. On the first tier, pupils may be asked to find out basic information on Lalique such as dates, country of origin, where he worked and the materials he worked with, alongside some pictures or sketches of one of his pieces. They may be provided with a fact sheet on the art nouveau movement and be asked to find images of examples from that era in other art forms such as glass. The second tier may require pupils of average ability to do the same thing as tier one but to show a use of tone, pattern, colour and texture in the drawings that they do. Attention may also be paid to the composition or layout on the pages of the research handed in. The more able pupils, or tier three, may be given the same sort of work in terms of research and drawing/composition but the task of finding out **how** Lalique worked and to say **how** his style 'fitted in' with the art movement of the time requires them to use higher order thinking skills. They may also be asked to comment on the scale and intricacy of his work and compare and contrast it with that of other jewellers or metal artists working at that time, or of a contemporary jeweller such as Erickson Beamon's headpieces.

As previously mentioned, the way the homework is set and worded is vitally important as able pupils should be expected to do slightly different work to others rather than more work than others. Young people are not stupid – they will know exactly why the teacher is giving them 'different' homework and will 'rank' themselves within the group very quickly without a word from the teacher! The teacher should therefore, make perfectly clear that there is no reason why pupils cannot be given the next tier up once they have mastered certain skills – being talented in one aspect of art and design does not mean they are talented in all other aspects. If they can analyse and evaluate well within the critical studies context, it doesn't mean to say they can draw fantastically well or control acrylic paint, for example. The argument for this practice of differentiation by task is that by simply giving everyone the same 'diet', some will fall behind as they will find the work too difficult or some will find it far too easy – both groups may then give up making the effort.

By dialogue

For example – Year 9: pupils are working on a large-scale batik based upon the designs and patterns found in Celtic art with an artist-in-residence. They have been given a day off timetable to dedicate to this special activity, although the artist is working on her own pieces all through the week and pupils can see her working and chat to her anytime they wish. The students have never worked on this scale before and have only just been introduced to batik processes, tools and materials. Throughout the day, the artist-in-residence uses specialist language to discuss what she wants them to achieve by the end. The teacher has quietly informed her who the more able pupils are in the group and at certain times during the day the artist discusses with them how they could extend and develop all the new techniques they have learned and allows them use of extra materials to experiment and explore batik to the full. The specialist language is constantly reinforced and pupils start to use it themselves very quickly. Some pupils make more progress than others and the artist encourages them to then refine their techniques with the wax and to experiment with the dyes to create different effects of colour and tone and to embellish sections with threads and specialist fabric pens.

By support

For example – Year 9:

Case study

Jennifer is a highly able student in most aspects of art, craft and design. She uses materials with confidence and maturity that would place her more at GCSE level than end of Key Stage 3 and her ability to discuss the subject in depth, explaining her thought processes and understanding of the work of a craftsperson for example, are constantly utilising higher order thinking skills without her knowing it! The only problem is Jennifer's behaviour in class. She has become extremely disruptive in lessons, her language is 'choice' and other pupils are beginning to resent the way she manages to stop them learning. The teachers constantly have to deal with her behaviour and time is being taken away from the support they can give other pupils. This is replicated in most of her lessons and she has found herself being put in the school's learning support unit for large parts of the day.

Jennifer now has the support of a learning mentor who is helping her with her emotional problems, most of which stem from her experiences outside of school, but she also has a teaching assistant to support her particularly with her artwork. The TA ensures that, through one-to-one support, Jennifer systematically works through the unit of work set by the art teacher who also supplies lesson plans specifically for her that are mainly differentiated by pace and task, due to Jennifer's high ability. She has an area of her own in the learning support unit and has been encouraged by the TA to set this up as a 'studio', displaying her work-in-progress on the walls, cut-outs from 'Tate' magazine to inspire her to keep up the good work and an individual action plan that is highly decorated by Jennifer's own sketches and in her direct line of vision. The TA has encouraged her to focus totally on the subject and in this way, has helped to calm her down in how she responds to teachers and her general behaviour.

Jennifer's work is regularly shown to the art teacher, as the TA is a non-specialist, in order for him to plan next steps. However, there is some flexibility in what Jennifer is allowed to do given the amount of time she is in the learning support unit and, as her favourite way of working is in three dimensions with clay, this structured, supportive, one-to-one environment ensures she can achieve to a high standard, experimenting with form, texture and pattern. She loves the work of Claes Oldenburg and has produced a wide variety of large-scale sculptures in clay and fabric relating to food, which have also impressed her peers! The support of the TA has been crucial in allowing her to think about art and design and not to feel she has to disrupt or distract constantly. Jennifer is gradually returning to normal timetabled lessons and still has a TA to support her back in the classroom. The TA has also been involved in all art departmental meetings and INSET and now has a base of knowledge that she did not before possess in the subject.

By pace

For example – Year 9 or 10: teachers could use the Getty Museum website to help in the planning of differentiation by pace for their more able students.

The website has an art education area (www.getty.edu/education), which provides lesson plans and curriculum ideas, image galleries and exhibitions, a teachers and learners online forum and a section that features recent exhibitions. It is an excellent site for art teachers of all key stages and able pupils from Key Stage 2 upwards. The section on lesson plans allows for differentiation by ability as well as age. This is very useful when planning for more able pupils as teachers can clearly see progression routes in one art appreciation skill area, for example personal expression in art making. This should help teachers to differentiate for the particular needs of just one pupil if necessary. Art and design as a subject covers a wide range of disciplines but art appreciation impacts upon all of them and in this respect, differentiating for the more able pupil can be quite time-consuming. By using this site, the teacher can easily locate where a student is currently at in his or her learning and then identify the next stage for further development, moving at a faster pace than the rest of the group or missing out some stages. This could be built into a unit of work or a lesson plan. Furthermore, the lesson plans section allows teachers to clearly see the next steps for their more able pupils.

The index of images is vast and each can be printed out for use in the classroom, or on worksheets, along with text. The information is broken down into contextual subheadings with examples of questions and activities for different 'age' groups but for this, the teacher should substitute 'ability groups'. That is, they would select materials from an older age group for able students.

More information on using the Getty site and other sites as a resource for Key Stage 3 or 4 can be found at www2.teachernet.gov.uk/gat, where there is a catalogue of resources that can be browsed by subject, key stage or teaching focus.

By content

For example – Years 7–9: every art department runs an art club of some description, after school, during dinner times on specified days of the week or as Easter or summer schools. These extracurricular sessions can prove to be a valuable chance for pupils to explore aspects of the subject that perhaps they cannot in normal lessons due to curriculum demands, length of lessons, etc. This activity can be covered over several art club sessions for Key Stage 3 able pupils, perhaps over a half term period of six weeks, and will allow them to extend their thinking about what art is and what feelings it conjures up in the viewer.

Key Stage 3 Able Pupils in Art and Design

Differentiation by Content

Curating a Virtual Exhibition

1. Pupils will start by creating self-portraits in a range of media such as collage, drawing, print and silk painting. The scale should vary from child to child and guidance should be given by the teacher as to appropriateness of scale in relation to the medium selected. This may be a continuation of work done in lesson time (*3 sessions*).

2. Pupils may use the Internet to look at gallery websites such as:

   - the National Portrait Gallery in London (www.npg.org.uk)

   - the National Gallery in London (www.nationalgallery.org.uk)

   - the Tate Galleries (www.tate.org.uk)

   to find examples of self-portraits by past and present artists that cover a range of media including photography, and select up to ten images that appeal to them to put in their 'virtual' exhibition. Pupils should make written or tape recorded notes on why they like these portraits and why they would be appropriate to sit alongside their own self-portraits they completed previously. Teacher support should be given as to the 'look' of the exhibition or the use of a theme to help pupils to be more selective (*1 session*).

3. Pupils will finalise their selection and produce an A1 or A2 presentation board to advertise the exhibition that should include an image of their own work. They might give the exhibition a title and write an introduction panel that summarises the reasons behind the selection of works, etc. such as one would see upon entering a real-life exhibition in a gallery. The teacher may also set up a facility for pupils to chat via telephone or email, to an education curator at a local gallery at a specified time, in order to get 'expert' feedback/guidance on their approaches (*2 sessions*).

By independence or responsibility

For example – Year 10/11: all pupils will be set a project brief by their teacher as part of their exam coursework. Teacher planning for the more able student should allow pockets of time, say near the beginning, middle and towards the end of the project, for that pupil to develop their work in their own direction and to build upon their particular individual strengths. These times should emphasise both quality and quantity and teacher input should be avoided unless absolutely necessary. Direct support can be given at other times, thus allowing pupils 'free flight' with their thoughts and ideas at prescribed times as appropriate to each individual pupil. The teacher may dedicate a particular area of the classroom to assist in this process, calling it 'The Free-Flight Area' and insisting upon creating an atmosphere there that is conducive to the flow of ideas. This type of differentiation does not only apply to Key Stage 4 – able pupils of all key stages will benefit from this process. See Appendix 4.1 for a lesson observation pro forma.

Effective questioning techniques

The use of higher order questioning with more able pupils allows the teacher to differentiate from questions that require lower order responses from the rest of the group without excluding them. If questions posed are constantly 'too easy' then pupils will stop answering. The effectiveness of questioning in teacher–pupil interactions can be significantly enhanced by a few basic techniques.

1. Pose the question first, before asking a pupil to respond

- When you call on a pupil before posing the question, the rest of the class is less likely to listen to the question, much less formulate a response.

- Posing the question before identifying someone to respond lets pupils know they will be held accountable and should be prepared to answer every question.

2. Allow plenty of 'think time' by waiting at least seven to ten seconds before expecting pupils to respond

- Ask pupils to refrain from responding until you ask for a volunteer or identify someone.

- Since most teachers wait only one to three seconds before expecting a response, the increased wait time can seem like an eternity and feel very uncomfortable at first.

- To help pupils adjust to an extended wait time, use the time to repeat and rephrase the question; also suggest that pupils use the time to write down the responses they compose.

3. Make sure you give all pupils the opportunity to respond rather than relying on volunteers

- Create a system to help you keep track of whom you call on, so you can ensure that all pupils have equal opportunities to contribute.

- If you call on a pupil who is not ready to respond or does not know the answer, allow the him/her to "pass" and then give her/him another opportunity later.

4. Hold pupils accountable by expecting, requiring, and facilitating their participation and contributions

- **Never** answer your own questions! If the pupils know you will give them the answers after a few seconds of silence anyway, what is their incentive?

- Do **not** accept 'I don't know' for an answer.

- Allow additional think time, if necessary, by moving on and then coming back to the pupil for a response later.

- Offer hints or suggestions to guide pupils in formulating quality responses.

- If a pupil is unable or unwilling to formulate a response, then offer two or more options and let them choose one.

5. Establish a safe atmosphere for risk-taking by guiding pupils in the process of learning from their mistakes

- **Always** 'dignify' incorrect responses by saying something positive about their efforts; public embarrassment only confirms apprehensions about class participation.

- When pupils make mistakes, build their confidence and trust by asking follow-up questions designed to help them self-correct and achieve success.

- Admit your own mistakes and 'think aloud' examples of a reflection process that demonstrates increased awareness, new insights, concept clarification, etc.

Homework

Why is homework still called 'homework'? Not a trick question, but could there be a more off-putting word?! 'Work' (without financial benefit!) is such a negative word to a lot of teenagers that it is a wonder we still use it. If we replace all references to 'work' with 'learning' it conjures up something much more constructive and meaningful within the school context. So . . . 'home learning' . . .

Home learning is necessary for all pupils if the full extent of the curriculum is to be met. Otherwise there just simply aren't enough hours in the day. For art and design curriculum coverage, home learning is essential in order for pupils to extend and enrich their learning and to pursue pathways at a more advanced level, but also to give specific time to improve the quality of their work and to add further enjoyment to doing the subject. Most schools use planners now that enable pupils to write down exactly what is required for them to do at home, and also add the date it is due to be handed in for marking. It is also advisable to put a home learning sheet together for pupils to take with them, as sometimes there is not enough space in the planner to write everything down. The DfES Standards site gives guidance on the format of what schools should reasonably expect students to do at home. Departments should ensure that:

- there is a clear policy statement, developed in consultation with the pupils, staff, parents and governors, and this is reviewed on a regular basis

- staff and pupils regard home learning as an integral part of the curriculum – it is planned and prepared alongside all other programmes of learning

- the foundations of effective home learning practices are established early on and develop progressively across the key stages – effective home learning practices can also be used to support effective transitionary links to the secondary phase

- home learning is set and managed effectively and contributes to the challenge of raising attainment

- home learning tasks are differentiated and are appropriate to the needs of individuals

- the support of parents and carers is seen as essential. They assist in many ways, for example, helping their children at home, monitoring home learning, providing encouragement, and even assisting with the marking of home learning

- effective home learning strategies support a range of settings in which pupils learn, for example, through parental support and guidance, joint family learning tasks, to independent learning

- home learning is marked according to the general school marking policy

- the quality of completed home learning is monitored and reviewed at regular periods in consultation with pupils and parents

- home learning completed well is acknowledged and praised

- innovative home learning practices that reflect developments within education and the range of learning styles (VAK, multiple intelligences), for example, the use of ICT, and 'accelerated learning'.

For able pupils' provision, an art department home learning policy could include a separate section that highlights what the department expects of this particular group:

Home learning task sheets – these will include compulsory home learning tasks for all pupils as well as optional extension learning. All pupils may complete the extension learning if they wish. Highly able pupils will be expected to complete the extension work as directed by their teacher and may even require different tasks to be set especially for them, which may replace some elements of the compulsory tasks. Teacher guidance will be given on this.

Marking – because of the project-based nature of this department's art, craft and design work, teachers may, if they wish, just write comments on Post-it notes on more able pupils' home learning (i.e. not give a mark). There will naturally be a blurring of boundaries between learning done in class and that done at home. This will take time to embed with a majority of pupils but the more able should find it common practice by Year 8. Therefore, marking should also cross the boundaries with work reviewed and marked at specific points rather than separating class and home learning. Pupils will need to be informed as to the school's marking system and will need regular feedback regarding their progress.

Feedback – pupils should hand in their home learning regularly to teachers in order to receive feedback and guidance. On some occasions, more able pupils may wish to lead 'round table' discussions on learning completed at home, rather than the teacher always taking the lead. The teacher may offer guidance at certain points in order to clarify or question but it has been found by this department to be one of the preferred and most effective ways of 'marking' and in involving all pupils in analysing and evaluating.

Sketchbooks and recording

The use of a sketchbook plays a vital part in enabling pupils to 'record observations and ideas, and collect visual evidence and information'.

The sketchbook provides the opportunity to:

- collect thoughts and ideas

- create a personal, private and shared resource

- use for observational work, working out ideas, record studies from imagination

- use as a starting point from which to develop large scale work

- use for experimenting with materials and techniques

- follow the established practice of artists

- contain evidence of gallery visits, working with artists, etc.

- work both inside and outside

- monitor progress and development

- develop a resource of ideas to inform further work.

The sketchbook may contain drawings, pieces of fabric, cuttings from magazines, postcards, mind maps, information about artists, computer-generated images, photographs and may include the use of a variety of graded pencils, pens, crayons, pastels, inks, a range of paints, etc.

The sketchbook is not a 'best' book but can of course contain finished pieces of work. For the able pupil, as with all pupils, it may be a source of great pride and ownership.

It is also important for the head of department to keep a portfolio of exemplar artwork across all art forms both two- and three-dimensional (where space is an

issue, photographs of three-dimensional work will suffice). It is a good idea to do this, especially to enable other staff and of course, pupils (links with Assessment for Learning) to see examples of perhaps different levels at Key Stage 3 and examples of grades in GCSE but in the case of able pupils it is advisable to keep pieces of work that perhaps show high ability but that do not fit in with level descriptors or 'perfect fit' GCSE grades. The teacher may decide to keep an example of a Level 6 piece of work if it was done by a Year 7 pupil or a piece by an able pupil who was entered for GCSE in advance of their years. Exemplar work can also act as a way of raising aspirations in pupils or those at risk of underachieving.

CHAPTER 5

Support for learning

- Support for more able pupils with learning difficulties
- Working with the support of learning mentors, teaching assistants and the pastoral team
- The school library
- Links with parents or guardians

Support for more able pupils with learning difficulties

The number and profile of pupils with special educational needs will vary from school to school, so it is important to consider the pupil with SEN as an individual within your school and subject environment.

There is a continuum of need within each of the selection of special educational needs listed here. Some pupils will be affected more than others, and show fewer or more of the characteristics described. The availability and levels of support from professionals within a school (e.g. SENCOs, support teachers, teaching assistants) and external professionals (e.g. educational psychologists, Learning Support Service staff, medical staff) will depend on the severity of the pupils' SEN. This continuum of need will also impact on the subject teacher's planning and allocation of support staff.

It is still important however, to recognise the individual pupil's particular high ability in art and design on a par with the other pupils in the group (sometimes the fact they are SEN pupils does not apply at all as the level of ability is so high; it also encourages full inclusion in lessons without constantly drawing attention to their particular 'need' amongst other pupils) and to encourage them to further improve their skills in this area whilst giving them as many opportunities as possible to extend their expertise into other aspects of the subject. This will require more considered planning on the part of the teacher, as special considerations will have to be incorporated.

Attention deficit disorder (with or without hyperactivity) – ADD/ADHD

Attention deficit hyperactivity disorder is a term used to describe children who exhibit over-active behaviour and impulsivity and who have difficulty in paying attention. This is a caused by a form of brain dysfunction of a genetic nature. ADHD can sometimes be controlled effectively by medication. Children of all levels of ability can have ADHD.

The main characteristics are:

- difficulty in following instructions and completing tasks
- easily distracted by noise, movement of others, objects attracting attention
- often doesn't listen when spoken to
- fidgets and becomes restless, can't sit still
- interferes with other pupils' work
- can't stop talking, interrupts others, calls out
- runs about when inappropriate
- has difficulty in waiting or taking turns
- acts impulsively without thinking about the consequences.

How can the art teacher help the able pupil with ADHD?

- make eye contact and use the pupil's name when speaking to him/her
- keep instructions simple – the one sentence rule
- demonstrate what you want him/her to do
- provide clear routines and rules, rehearse them regularly
- sit the pupil away from obvious distractions e.g. windows, store cupboard, computer
- in busy situations direct the pupil by name to visual or practical objects, materials or tools
- encourage the pupil to repeat back instructions before starting work
- tell the pupil when to begin a task
- give two choices; avoid the option of the pupil saying 'no', for example: 'Do you think pencil or fineliner would be the best to use here?'
- give advanced warning when something is about to happen, change or finish with a time, for example, 'in two minutes I need you (pupil name) to . . .'
- give specific praise – catch him/her being good, give attention for positive behaviour or taking care with work

- give the pupil responsibilities so that others can see him/her in a positive light and he/she develops a positive self-image, e.g. demonstrate to other pupils how he/she has done something in his/her art or craftwork that worked particularly well, such as expressive use of a particular medium; handling and control of materials when working on a large scale.

When working with pupils with SEN, and especially a pupil with ADHD, it is of utmost importance to ensure that health and safety rules apply at all times. Teachers should re-emphasise this with any support staff given the practical nature of the subject and requisite to use specialist tools and materials. Points to note include these safety tips:

- Round-nosed and a choice of right and left-handed scissors should be available in the art room.

- Glue used should be a washable PVA where necessary or a low-temperature electric glue gun.

- PVA is a suitable substitute for varnish. If varnish is used, supervision is necessary.

- Incising polystyrene may be done with biros rather than sharp tools.

- Printing inks should be non-toxic and water-based.

- Care must be taken with the handling of mirrors – reflective plastic tiles are a suitable alternative.

- Water-soluble non-toxic inks and paints must be an alternative within the art room.

- Sharp metallic objects or chicken wire may require gloves and goggles to be worn.

- Great care should be taken when using hot wax (batik) – ensure all flexes are taped down to avoid accidents and that pupils are supervised at all times including when handling dyes.

- There should be supervision of the cutting of doweling. The wearing of goggles may be appropriate when handling willow or canes.

Safety tips relating to specific projects should be displayed around the room and attention drawn to them verbally and visually at the beginning of each lesson. Some SEN pupils may require continued support from a teaching or classroom assistant throughout.

Asperger syndrome

Case study – Lucy

Lucy is a tall, very attractive girl who has been variously labelled as having Asperger and 'cocktail party syndrome'. She talks fluently but usually about something totally irrelevant. She is very charming and her language is sometimes quite sophisticated but her ability to use language for schoolwork in Year 10 operates at a much lower level. Her reading is excellent on some levels but she cannot draw inferences from the printed word. If you ask her questions about what she has read, she looks blank, echoes what you have said, looks puzzled or changes the subject – something she is very good at.

She finds relationships quite difficult. She is very popular, especially with the boys in her class. They think she is a laugh. There have been one or two problems with some of the boys in her school. Her habit of standing too close to people and her over-familiarity has led to misunderstandings that have upset her. Her best friend Sarah is very protective of her and tries to mother her, to the extent of doing some of her work for her so she won't get into trouble.

Her work is limited. In art, all her pictures look the same, very small cramped drawings but ones which are highly detailed and on many occasions she has been able to recall minute details and draw them accurately, which others may have missed completely. She does not like to use paint because it is 'messy'. She finds it very hard to relate to the wider world and sees everything in terms of her own experience. The class have been studying Macbeth and she has not moved beyond saying, 'I don't believe in witches and ghosts'.

Some teachers think she is being wilfully stupid or not paying attention. She seems to be attention-seeking as she is very poor at turn taking and shouts out in class if she thinks of something to say or wants to know how to spell a word. When she was younger, she used to retreat under the desk when she was upset and had to be coaxed out. She is still easily offended and cannot bear being teased. She has an answer for everything and while it may not be sensible or reasonable, there is an underlying logic.

Strategies to assist Lucy in the art lesson

- To help her become more independent – try using computer software in art lessons in the first instance, which is not 'messy', in order for Lucy to achieve in a different medium. Animation packages such as *Kar2ouche* (Immersive Education) allow the manipulation of given images which will help to build confidence, but students can combine these with their own drawings or designs, given or recorded sounds, which make the whole experience more personal. There is *Kar2ouche* software on 'Macbeth' (one of many titles in many subject areas), which may help Lucy in her English lessons also.

- To count to 20 before shouting out – when teaching the whole class, allow thinking time for responses that is, in most cases, longer than eight seconds (which feels like a long time!) so that all students are required to think before responding – again, not making Lucy's 'counting' time so obvious.

- Move her away from Sarah – perhaps next to another female student whose drawing skills aren't as highly developed as Lucy's and encourage occasional peer tutoring.

- Writing frames and examples of past students' work that she can model her responses on.

- Discussion of social issues, body language, appropriate behaviour, etc. – for example, this can be done in a unit of work via critical analysis of work by artists, sculptors, designers and makers which prompt discussion and provoke thought, such as the work of Salvador Dali.

- Promote experimentation in lessons, especially in sketchbooks, gradually increasing scale, new materials and techniques, but allowing time for Lucy to continue with small-scale drawings if she wishes and perhaps introducing other skills and areas which require attention to detail such as jewellery or highly-worked textiles.

Dyslexia

Case study – Michael

Michael obtained a place at a boys' grammar school but has struggled ever since. He has an extensive vocabulary and always volunteers for drama productions and reporting back when working in a group. He enjoys music, art and D&T and brings a keen imagination and wit to all these subjects. Michael prefers the company of teachers and older pupils with whom he likes to debate topical issues. His peers, on the other hand, regard him as a 'bit of a wimp' as he does not enjoy sport and frequently corrects their behaviour.

After a very slow start in early childhood, Michael can now read fluently but his other problems associated with dyslexia remain. His spelling and handwriting are very poor. He finds it almost impossible to obtain information from large swathes of text. Even when the main ideas are summarised for him in bullet points, he has difficulty revising for examinations or tests or picking out and organising the main ideas for an essay. In maths, he is criticised for the chaotic layout of his work but he finds it difficult to organise things in a way that is logical to other people. His family is very supportive and give him a lot of help with homework, so much so that teachers are sometimes misled into believing that he is coping well, until his difficulties are highlighted by his very poor performance in written exams. Because he is so articulate, Michael is able to explain his frustrations to his teachers who are, on the whole, sympathetic. However, they're not always very helpful in providing him with useful strategies.

Strategies for art and design

- Liaise with the learning support team so that your approach with Michael fits in with their overall support programme for him.

- Teach Michael to use mind maps so that he can record information and plan his work if he finds this helpful.

- Encourage him to record his thoughts and ideas by making audio recordings or setting them to music.

- Make sure that home learning tasks are suitable for his level of ability but are modified to allow him to succeed. For example, give him a template of notes or a research framework with keywords missing rather than asking him to make his own notes when researching an artist or art movement.

- Encourage him to word process some homework, insisting on careful use of a spellchecker if a written piece is necessary. However, teachers should concentrate on annotation of sketchbook work, where spelling corrections are made and discussed with Michael but in no way detract from his actual art, craft or design work set.

The following project outline provides opportunities to build on Michael's strengths and develop weaker ones.

Art and design project – 'About Collage'

Objectives

- to make the most of Michael's keen imagination and wit in a project that will extend all pupils' skills of literacy through a play on words

- to expand upon their collage and compositional skills but to emphasise the need for accuracy and tidiness in the presentation of a two-dimensional final piece in order for their work to fit onto a side of A4 or smaller

- to consider collage as an illustrative technique.

Activities

1. Home learning – pupils think about a hobby or pastime they particularly enjoy participating in, or a subject they know a lot about or feel passionate about. The teacher asks them to bring in an assortment of loose cut-outs from magazines/photocopies from specialist books or cut-outs from images off the internet (any scale/size, in colour or black and white, etc.) that relate to their chosen subject.

2. In class, the teacher discusses composition and layout, perhaps touching on the rules of perspective but not allowing that to be the main focus. There is discussion about how using collage techniques can help with composition by placing objects, people, backgrounds, etc., in different positions until the best layout of balance and structure is achieved. Some painters use this method for planning their paintings and leave elements of collage in the painting to create texture.

   I use it [collage] as a medium that may or may not be left out of the painting. I work out a painting in a flexible way with collage. I can try things out and change them. Quite early on I decided I liked the purity of single washes of paint rather than a broken surface, so with collage I avoid over-working. I accumulated great sacks of colour in bits of paper. When

I began to use them, the picture would call for different colours and then I would know what colours to mix in paint. It was as if I waited for the picture to talk to me – to tell me what it wanted. You look at the picture and it sort of asks something.

(Sandra Blow)

3. Pupils select figurative and non-figurative images from magazines provided by the teacher and construct different compositions in their sketchbooks that use mainly collage, but restricting them to limited use of coloured pencils, paint, etc., to 'fill in' gaps or backgrounds. The theme for these should still be the pupils' identified special interest.

4. The teacher leads further discussions and provides pictorial examples of the work of modern artists who have used collage in their work, such as Raoul Hausmann's *The Art Critic* (1919–20), Richard Hamilton's *Just What Is It That Makes Today's Homes So Different, So Appealing?* (1956), Kurt Schwitters' *Picture of Spatial Growths – Picture With Two Small Dogs* (1939) and Peter Blake's *Sgt Pepper* album cover. Pupils then adapt and refine their preliminary work in sketchbooks following further analysis and small-group discussions of these images. The teacher should ask pupils to introduce limited text (collage or written form) to their ideas that perhaps highlights specific aspects of their chosen subject area.

5. Pupils create a final collage that depicts their chosen subject or hobby.

6. The teacher shows examples to the class of Graham Rawle's collages, in particular his *Lost Consonants* or *Vowel Movements* series as featured in *The Guardian Weekend* magazine. This contemporary use of wit within the medium of collage should particularly appeal to Michael. The play on words is discussed in small groups and pupils work in pairs to create a sentence or phrase in a similar style.

7. Pupils then create their own individual small-scale collage that incorporates their sentence or phrase, with the emphasis being on control of materials as well as a witty punchline!

8. Pupils make written or recorded notes that evaluate the way their work has altered since the start of the project and suggest successful techniques they may use again in the future, plus areas that need further refinement.

Useful resources

Modern Artists Series: Peter Black (2003) by Natalie Rudd (London: Tate)

The 20th Century Art Book: Mini Version (1996) by Susannah Lawson (London: Phaidon Press)

www.tate.org.uk

www.grahamrawle.com

Examples of collage in different contexts

Joseph Cornell's assemblages, for example *Untitled* (1950, private collection)

Tracey Emin's textile collages, for example *There's a Lot of Money in Chairs* (1994, appliquéd armchair)

Working with the support of learning mentors, teaching assistants and the pastoral team

Why should pupils of high ability need mentoring? Well, because they may have particular social and emotional needs, which may need support:

- difficulties with peers

- expectations of teachers and parents: must be aware that emotional maturity is not always in line with intellectual ability and not to expect too much all the time

- decision-making and perfectionism – aid children to make appropriate choices and develop a sense of proportion

- intellectual arrogance – help children to see the advantages of an open mind and broader perspective and develop their skills for effective teamwork

- feelings of isolation and/or anxiety – help them to develop perspective and a positive view of self.

Mentoring can be seen as a means of providing stimulating and worthwhile experiences for children of high ability. There are three different forms of mentoring and these do not necessarily need to be carried out specifically by a learning mentor. They are:

1. academic mentoring – learning related issues

2. holistic mentoring – academic or social issues

3. occupational mentoring – workplace related experience and information.

The key to successful mentoring is to identify the purpose of the mentoring. This needs to be done by both the mentor and mentee. The mentor may then use questioning as a way of promoting higher order thinking within that process.

The case study below is from a report from a real school in Merseyside, although names have been changed for obvious reasons. It highlights the impact that successful teamwork between the learning mentor, school staff and the willingness of the able but underachieving pupil can make in turning one pupil around at a crucial stage in their lives with support, understanding and creative thinking!

Learning mentor case study

In January 2001, learning mentors were employed at Anytown Community High School as part of the national Excellence in Cities strategy. Initially it was decided that they should focus on two specific areas, attendance and one-to-one work with Year 11 pupils. This was agreed for three reasons:

1. It was half way through the academic year.

2. To publicise the mentoring role to staff, pupils and parents.

3. To set up systems within school.

The aims were:

- to raise attendance
- to raise awareness
- to remove barriers to learning
- to assist individual pupils to reach their full potential.

Chris

Chris lives in Anytown with his parents. His mother is a housewife and his father is a van driver. He has two older siblings – a brother who lives away from home and a sister who is 19 and lives very close to the family with her partner and one-year-old child.

Chris is a typical adolescent boy. He does not talk easily about himself and looks quite sullen. He does not wear full school uniform and often wears a baseball cap in school. He is usually polite and well mannered.

His GCSE grades had slipped at Christmas, from potential Grade As to possible Grade Ds. Chris was very disaffected. Both staff and the learning mentor felt that he was in danger of dropping out of school altogether. Chris was late to school every morning.

One-to-one interviews between Chris and his learning mentor

05.01.01 Time spent filling in personal statement for his National Record of Achievement. Talked about his attendance (94%) and the fact that he is always late.

15.01.01 Filled in an individual action plan aimed at helping Chris identify and prioritise areas in specific subjects where he needed support.

05.03.01 Talked to Chris about mentoring and what it means. Also discussed his work experience, which he had not enjoyed. The learning mentor sent out an interim behaviour report for staff to fill in. Discussed the fact that his projected grades had dropped from A to D – he was positive he would get at least Bs.

16.03.01 Helped Chris to fill in a personal evaluation exercise. He scored very low on self-motivation. Chris's main interest was art, especially graphic design, so the Learning Mentor arranged for him to have a one-day work experience at a graphic design company based in Manchester. It was a small company which produced literature for Manchester Airport and the Lowry. The ultimate aim was to motivate Chris.

23.03.01 The learning mentor discussed the work experience and how she hoped he would behave and dress.

03.04.01 The work experience in Manchester. Chris arrived at 8.45am (15 minutes early) dressed smartly, with art coursework to do if he had time! He was shown basic graphics programs on the computer and given a small design task to do that lasted the whole day. At the end of the day designers gave him extra guidance with the coursework he had brought along. They completed a short report for the school, which Chris brought back with him.

(Whilst on this work experience the learning mentor received the behaviour reports back from school staff with comments that included 'very poor behaviour', 'always late', and 'distracts other pupils'.)

26.04.01   The learning mentor discussed the success of Chris's work experience and an incident in school, which he was particularly upset about. She then spoke to his art teacher about his attitude in lessons towards the teacher, his peers, his class and homework, and passed on all the information and feedback from his work experience.

Chris had thoroughly enjoyed his one-day work experience. He also started to talk more openly as he seemed to have renewed confidence in his ability.

03.05.01   Chris didn't attend his interview with the learning mentor as he was very late coming into school.

14.05.01   Chris's last interview with the learning mentor where they talked about goal setting and as he was confident that he would do well, how he could achieve his goals. Together they ensured applications were filled in for sixth form colleges in the area and the learning mentor posted these.

Conclusion

1. Chris's attitude changed over the course of interviews with the learning mentor, starting with the fact that he apologised to school staff if he was late.

2. He attended two study days over the Easter holidays to finish coursework.

3. He came into school on time on twenty occasions during March and April. Before this January was the last time he had arrived on time.

4. He was accepted on an Oxford University summer school for a week and the gifted and talented coordinator based at the university nominated him for a special prize.

5. He arrived early for every exam dressed in full school uniform, a bright white shirt and shoes not trainers.

6. His art coursework and exam were completed to a very high standard and were submitted on time, however he did leave it to the teacher to mount and present all his work for the moderation! He gained a grade A.

One member of staff commented, when the learning mentor was checking if Chris was in school before a modular science exam, 'He will be here because he is so well motivated'.

There is no doubt by staff at Anytown Community High School that without the support and guidance of the learning mentor, and without her 'thinking-out-of-the-box' approach i.e. coming up with the idea of organising for him a more meaningful work experience, Chris would not have turned around as quickly as he did. He just needed someone to have faith in him and to really listen to what he enjoyed doing.

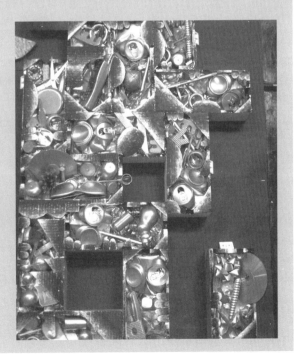

The school library

As well as equipping the art department with subject-specific resources that more able pupils have access to when in lessons or art club, the school library also needs materials for reference if pupils require access at other times. School libraries should be stocked with appealing books (not just tired-looking ones that seem like they have been there for decades! No-one will look at them!). They ought to address a wide range of art movements and genres, making sure that areas such as medieval and Renaissance art and contemporary art are included as these are often not well catered for in secondary schools (Downing and Watson 2004). Cultures and traditions also need to be represented as well as crafts and sculpture. Funding for these resources is always a concern for heads of art but a good library collection can be built up over time. As teachers plan ahead for the coming year, they may be able to budget for three or four key books that will assist in able pupils' learning. ICT facilities are a big feature in school libraries nowadays and as well as authorised internet access, pupils who are more able in art may require the use of particular software in order to do 'home learning'. When purchasing software such as 'Adobe Photoshop', schools usually buy a site licence as well, which allows it to be networked across all PCs in the school, so that pupils can use it in the art department and the school library, as well as ICT suites in other parts of the school.

When purchasing for the library, heads of department may wish to think about what exactly they will require able pupils to learn or find out about over the academic year, as opposed to those of more average ability. Resources that help to encourage the use of higher order thinking skills, allow for depth and breadth of research and cover all aspects of art, craft and design to allow ideas to flourish should be provided.

Links with parents or guardians

These are vital to ensure that the able pupil in art and design has continuity of support from home to school and vice versa. As mentioned previously, parents and guardians can assist with home learning and providing space to work. At parents' evenings, teachers can emphasise what learning routes they have planned for the children, discuss progress with individual action plans and can highlight and explain the child's particular ability in art. It is always useful to have a list of careers in art and design handy for parents to take away with them – so often can be heard comments along the lines of 'But what can he/she do with a qualification in art?!'

Parents or guardians may be art, craft or design specialists in their own right and could be in a position to offer their expertise directly to able pupils. Obviously they would have to be police-checked first but usually they are willing to give of their time as much as possible. They could lead classroom workshops or work with smaller groups out-of-school hours, for example. They might be able to provide links with businesses and other organisations to enhance classroom provision, including access to experts in their field. Involve them in their child's education – it is well worth it!

Working with artists-in-residence

Work produced by students and a digital artist-in-residence for the 'Chartres' project discussed in Chapter 6

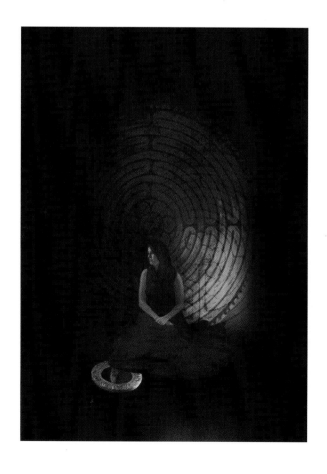

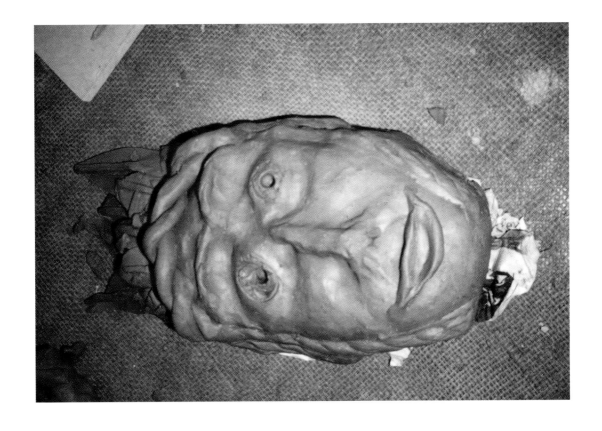

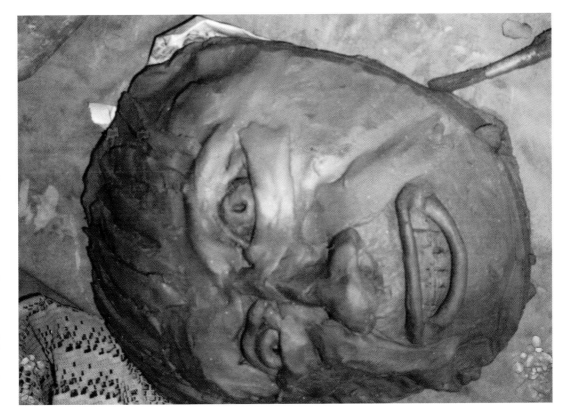

Year 7 clay portraits produced during artist residency

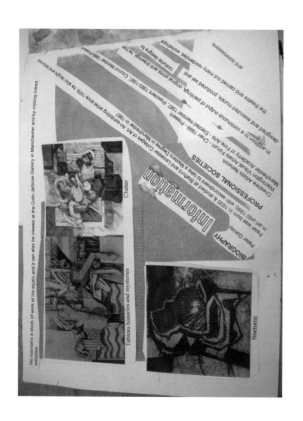

Able pupils working outside the classroom as extension and enrichment

Masterclass at Liverpool John Moores University

Examples of work by able pupils in Years 9, 10 and 11

Textile pieces based on Pop Art and Identity

Research on African and Indian art and artefacts

Examples of large-scale card sculptures

Textile work

CHAPTER 6

Beyond the classroom

- Visits
- Links with other organisations
- Summer schools in art, craft and design
- Masterclasses

Experience of art, craft and design outside the classroom is absolutely essential in the learning of all pupils, not just the more able. The subject is a wonderful living organism that needs to be experienced within many different contexts to enhance its life outside of school and to particularly allow more able pupils to make it part of their lives.

> I do believe that art should be deep pleasure and a part of everyone's life. I do not think we can live without art of some form. I think I would be quite mad without it.
>
> (David Hockney)

Similarly, art teachers also need regular injections of subject-specific INSET, gallery visits, artist-in-residencies, masterclasses and links with outside organisations to remain 'healthy' and to remain part of the art world, not just the teaching world.

Visits

In art and design, visits to art galleries and places of inspirational interest are a vital part of curriculum provision, just as much as in a subject such as geography (field trips) or English literature (live performances). The feeling of seeing a painting or sculpture 'in the flesh' really cannot be beaten. We would not be art teachers if we hadn't had moments like mocking reproduction Monet's in furniture shops, then seeing the real, full scale paintings and feeling the atmosphere in them at the Musée de l'Orangerie and being gob-smacked; or walking through Yorkshire Sculpture Park and amongst the trees you catch sight of Antony Gormley's standing figure at the top of a huge tree trunk which takes your breath away, or similarly having to move out of the way for Sally Matthews' 'Wild Boar Clearing' at Grizedale Forest – awesome! It is that experience that we all need to feel at least once in our lives and for more able children in art, craft and design it is vital. We must offer able pupils as many opportunities as we can to allow them to feel this.

It is a good idea to register your school on the mailing lists of as many art and craft galleries and sculpture parks as possible so that visits to exhibitions can be fully incorporated into lesson planning and units of work.

The planning sheets on pages 84 and 85 outline a unit of work that incorporates a visit to a gallery as an integral part and not as a stand-alone trip without foundation or follow-on. (The planning sheets can also be found on the accompanying CD.)

Despite the fact that taking pupils off-site for educational trips and visits is becoming more and more time-consuming for teachers in the planning and preparation stage, given the amount of risk assessments that need to be carried out beforehand and forms filled in, the enormous benefits on learning and art appreciation by visiting galleries and the like cannot be underestimated and ought to be viewed as an essential element of the curriculum at all Key Stages.

Links with other organisations

Case study – a graphic design competition organised with a local business

The head of art and design at the school approached a local large Indian food manufacturing company with the initial idea. They felt this was a good way of making further links with the local community and consulted their design team, who wrote a brief asking pupils to build upon what they had learned about Pakistani and Indian designs and develop further designs for their sauce jars and any other publicity they may use to 'launch' the new designs.

The company supplied jars of sauces, display boards, design planning sheets, mock-up jar labels and information on the history of the company and its current place within the specialised 'authentic food' market. Two representatives of the company spoke to pupils during one of their lessons, treating them as the designers. The representatives were the customer and set the design brief and said it was to be a competition to create a winning design that best met the brief and emphasised and conveyed the 'authentic' feel of the product.

The head of art created a display with everything that had been given and when discussing the brief with pupils, explained about the use of logos and so on.

Half-way through the project the food company representatives came into a lesson to speak to the pupils about their ideas and to offer further information, guidance and support if needed to assist them in realising their intentions and meeting the design brief.

Before the end of term, designs were submitted to the company and they had a week to choose the 'best' four designs. In the meantime, pupils evaluated the project in their sketchbooks and through discussion. Most of the more able pupils had also designed promotional material and had taken advantage of the after-school art clubs to use ICT facilities and to work as a group to share ideas. This was optional to all pupils and those who attended were of varying ability but totally absorbed in the project.

The Indian food company's team came back into the art lesson a week later with a short-listed selection of submitted artwork. These pupils were then asked to discuss their designs and the team then decided upon the four winners. Two of the four were those officially identified as being more able in art and design, and the other two were of average ability but had excelled in this project. Each pupil received vouchers to buy books or art materials. One overall winner also had her design printed by the company and put on a tin and a sauce jar!

Case study – the 'Chartres' project

As part of a new initiative entitled 'Encore', BBC Radio 3 and the Royal Philharmonic Society set out to rediscover significant orchestral works by living composers. Fifteen works were performed by some of the country's leading orchestras in venues nationwide. The concerts were all broadcast on Radio 3 and each work was the subject of a specifically tailored outreach project designed to encourage wider audiences and greater understanding of the music.

For this particular combined art and music project, Liverpool's Anglican Cathedral played host to artwork created by six highly able pupils. The artwork added an extra dimension to Judith Bingham's orchestral work, 'Chartres'.

Art, craft and design medium-term planning: Key Stage 3

THEME/TOPIC: Textiles and Costume of Pakistan and India	YEAR GROUP: 9	CLASS: 9KE	TERM: 1	TIME ALLOCATION: 1 term

LEARNING OBJECTIVES

- To learn about the traditional textiles of Pakistan (and India) and the materials and processes used to make them.
- To have a greater understanding of pattern, colour, texture and decoration in Pakistani textiles and costume.
- To produce drawings of Pakistani or Indian costume and textiles combined with looking at and discussing styles, techniques and motifs for inspiration.
- To explore new techniques such as traditional block prints with fabric dyes/paints and experiment with stitching and use of a variety of materials such as small (plastic) mirrors on the fabric.
- To produce a small textile/mixed media piece using own choice of technique such as embroidery, quilting, dyeing, etc.
- Pupils study the work of twins Amrit and Rabindra Kaur Singh and discuss mix of modern and traditional Asian culture.
- *Link with business/competition into graphic design.
- *Visual, auditory and kinaesthetic learning styles will be covered in this project.*

PROJECT OUTLINE

- Pupils will study the traditional textiles and costumes of Pakistan (and India – more able).
- They will learn the techniques of block printing and painting with fabric dyes, quilting and stitching to embellish work.
- From secondary resources they will discuss the formal elements in association with these textiles and the teacher will incorporate *higher order thinking skills* into group work for more able pupils.
- **Pupils will visit the Victoria and Albert Museum in London to see traditional costumes first-hand and will make observational studies in a special sketchbook to be filled by the end of the project and to highlight the development of ideas and new techniques learned (Teacher: also research local galleries' and museums' collections).**
- Pupils will then create their own small-scale textile piece using mixed media and a variety of their chosen methods.
- Pupils discuss work of Kaur Singh twins.
- Pupils will take part in a competition with a local business (well-known brand of Indian foods), to design a range of new labels and publicity for their sauces.

CROSS-CURRICULAR LINKS
- PHSE
- textiles technology
- geography
- history
- RE
- citizenship

KEY VOCABULARY
- textiles
- pattern
- decoration
- colour
- texture
- elaborate
- detail
- graphic design
- embellish
- traditional
- contemporary
- costume

LEARNING OUTCOMES

Expectations at the end of this unit will be:

Must: all pupils will find out about textiles and costumes from Pakistan and India and make drawings in sketchbooks that include pattern, colour and texture from first (V&A visit) and second-hand resources (books and websites). They will produce a design of their own and create a small decorative panel using fabric or paper and other materials and newly learned techniques. They will look at the work of the Singh twins. They will produce designs for Indian cooking sauce jars, further developing and extending their ideas and techniques. They will realise their ideas and intentions.

Should: pupils should develop their ideas and techniques based upon their research and resources provided. Their designs will reflect their influences and their annotations will be clear throughout their sketchbooks. They will discuss and make connections between British and Asian cultures through the work of the Singh twins. They will use new techniques to extend their ideas into Graphic Design, creating designs and ideas for Indian food sauce labels and publicity.

Could: more able pupils could create highly detailed and well-planned designs for textiles on fabric and/or paper. Their work will reflect Pakistani or Indian traditional methods, colours, textures and some embellishments but will also incorporate their own ideas, thus extending their learning. They will discuss and evaluate their own work and make connections between their work and others. They will evaluate and comment upon the differences between Asian and British cultures and this will inform also their textile work. They may wish to further develop their artwork using ICT for the Graphic Design competition and print out labels and publicity to give a more professional finish.

HEALTH AND SAFETY:

In addition to the regular art department health and safety policy:

- Use of fabric dyes and paints
- Use of scissors to cut fabric, materials or paper for textile piece
- Use of sewing needles
- Copy of Risk Assessment needed from V & A, transport arrangements and travel insurance to and from London
- Member of school staff to be present at all times when on visit and working with others.
- Care with display of sauce jars as they are glass.

ASSESSMENT OPPORTUNITIES

- Ability to produce a design in class from observations of Pakistani and Indian costume and textiles and/or artefacts.
- Ability to develop an awareness of pattern, colour, texture and design.
- Ability to produce a design for textiles derived from Pakistani or Indian patterns, colours, methods and/or materials and successfully transfer that design onto fabric or paper.
- Homework tasks to include research of Indian patterns and architecture and development of ideas.
- Ability to adapt and refine ideas when changing to Graphic Design and using different methods and materials.
- Ability to produce final designs in graphics section.
- Ability to make contributions to discussions on culture, tradition, techniques (previously learned and new), methods and ideas.
- 'Judging' for competition by Indian food company's graphics and publicity team – meeting the design brief or surpassing it.
- Assessment of NC Levels met: 4–8.

DIFFERENTIATION

- By task, independence, pace, dialogue and outcome
- More able/less able may omit elements and will cover range of objectives
- More able extend into links with Indian art/artefacts and textiles
- Final textile piece is open-ended task allowing for limited to more able ability
- Connections made and built upon with Contemporary artists (especially more able)
- Individual help and support given during lesson time; differentiated home learning
- Transfer from Textiles to Graphics may require support

MATERIALS/RESOURCES

- *Colours of the Indus* by Nasreen Askari and Rosemary Crill (Merrell Holberton Press/V&A, 1997, ISBN 1 85894 044 3)
- *India Modern* by Herbert J.M. Ypma (Phaidon Press, 2000, ISBN 0714839485)
- *Twin Perspectives* – Paintings by Amrit and Rabindra KD Kaur Singh (Twin Studio, 1999, ISBN 0 9535 111 0 3)
- www.ists.qimr.edu.au/singh.html
- *Live at Carnegie Hall* Music CD of Anoushka Shankar (Angel Records, 2001)
- Fabric for printing on/decorating, quilting
- Fabric dyes or paints and pens
- Range of coloured threads, mirror decorations, sequins, sewing needles, etc.
- PVA glue
- Ranges of papers
- Watercolours/acrylics
- Range of grades of pencil, coloured pencils
- ICT facilities if required to manipulate designs, etc.
- A4 or A5 Sketchbooks
- Wooden printing blocks (teacher's own, bought from outlet in Rusholme, Manchester)

'Chartres' was inspired by the composer's visit to the French medieval cathedral, famous for its beautiful rose window. The pupils each chose a movement from the piece and then created their own visual interpretations. The project was a unique opportunity to link the selected school with a large organisation such as BBC Philharmonic (Martin Maris – Project Manager), who approached the able pupils consultant at the local authority in the first instance. A local secondary school was then selected which the consultant knew had a strong art department who wished to extend their ICT provision, and teamed them up with a digital artist, Dorrie Halliday. The six pupils spent a week off their normal timetable working with the artist-in-residence in the art department using:

- industry-standard digital imaging techniques that improved not only their knowledge of the programs but also improved their ability to conceive artistic practices using a digital format
- pre-production, production and post-production skills
- digital housekeeping
- scanning resolutions
- file formats
- printing problems
- saving dilemmas.

The pupils also developed their communication and team-building skills within the group. It was very constructive allowing them to bring in examples of their own work on the first day to show and discuss with Dorrie and the rest of the group, treating them as artists in their own right. Dorrie also asked them to bring in something that had inspired them to assist in the process of encouraging the pupils to talk about their ideas and to share techniques and to link in with the processes employed by the artist herself and the composer Judith Bingham.

The pupils were given copies of the music to take home and listen to and asked to explore their ideas via their sketchbooks. A day was spent becoming familiar with Adobe Photoshop software, in particular its layering techniques. As the pupils' ideas developed they had a clearer picture of their intended outcomes. Dorrie organised some models to come into school so that the pupils could photograph them in the best clothing and poses for their compositional images. These were then downloaded onto the computers to further enhance the nature of the work, incorporating figurative with non-figurative elements.

Once the final seven digital images were completed – one per pupil, plus one that Dorrie herself created – five were printed onto huge two by four metre full-colour banners and suspended from balconies inside the cathedral. At the performance of 'Chartres', these were lit appropriately as the music guided the audience around the building. The two remaining images were printed onto fabric which formed the costumes for a male and female dancer who performed during the piece.

Each pupil was allowed to keep their own banner or costume and these are on display within the school. The images were also turned into postcards, sets of which have been distributed nationwide and form a permanent feature in the portfolios of these six able pupils. (See the colour plate section and the accompanying CD for full-colour images.)

This was an extremely rewarding experience for all involved. There are other organisations that run outreach projects for art and design and many are self-funding. Some heads of art ask a member of their staff to take responsibility for seeking out these projects as part of extension and enrichment provision.

Providing a curriculum for more able pupils is not solely about one-off experiences such as this but as part of a rich artistic diet that is fundamentally based upon classroom provision. Projects like this will remain in their memories forever, inspiring and motivating them to continue to achieve to their full potential.

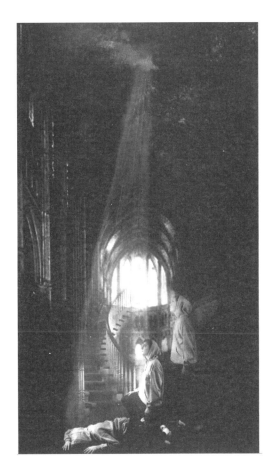 

Summer schools in art, craft and design

A variety of summer schools are on offer to more able pupils in art and design every year. These are usually run by:

- individual secondary schools either solely for their own pupils or with the addition of feeder primaries and other nearby secondaries

- specialist schools who use summer schools as a way of highlighting and sharing their particular expertise and often build in INSET for staff, possibly working alongside pupils

- local authorities (through subject-specialist advisers and consultants or gifted and talented coordinators) for pupils across the whole local area (usually Years 6–9) and that bring in experts in their field

- universities and colleges of further education in areas that extend and enhance classroom learning and utilise the specialist equipment that these institutions can offer such as flatbed print presses, fabric printing equipment, access to Apple Macs and specialist graphics packages, etc.

- specific organisations such as galleries and museums whose summer schools or courses are usually a series of one-off events and activities.

With all summer schools, places are obviously limited and dependent upon funding. If pupils do have to pay, then this is mostly a nominal fee and other funding bodies meet the rest of the costs. Each summer school will have its own criteria for selection or eligibility to attend and these are dependent upon staff/pupil ratios, individual ability and passion for the subject, teacher references (sometimes) and the aims and intended outcomes of the activities on offer. Very few are residential. The duration of summer schools can vary but they are generally at least a week and in most cases, no more than two.

Summer schools specifically for those with artistic talent should aim to:

- enrich and extend educational provision

- identify and motivate pupils, including those underachieving

- 'stretch' these children and enhance their educational achievement

- enrich their educational experience and/or enable them to engage early with material they would not normally encounter until later

- improve continuity and progression in their educational experience, including between the primary and secondary sector, not least by developing the knowledge and understanding of school staff

- promote access to higher education for able children from disadvantaged backgrounds

- promote effective partnership between maintained and independent schools

- improve the capacity of the schools involved to cater for more able pupils.

(Taken from the DfES guidance at www.standards.dfes.gov.uk/giftedandtalented/
guidanceandtraining/summerschoolguidance.)

Example: Year 11 'Young at Art' summer schools, University of the Arts London

The University of the Arts London opens its doors every summer to Year 11 pupils, to give them the opportunity to find out what life is really like at art college. This year (2005) they are hosting three summer schools:

1. a residential film and television school at London College of Communication
2. a residential fashion school at London College of Fashion
3. a non-residential art and design school at Camberwell College of Arts

Fashion school

In July 2004, the London College of Fashion and Central Saint Martins College of Art and Design welcomed sixty young people from across England for their Year 11 Fashion Summer School. Throughout the week the students were engaged in a variety of fashion-based activities including fashion illustration, fashion design, and body adornment. It was a creative and lively week and the students particularly enjoyed the chance to use the resources available in the colleges and work with a wide variety of materials and with mannequins to develop their designs.

Alongside the practical workshops, the students were given advice on careers by people working within the industry, and about building portfolios, interview skills and financing courses. Alongside the tutors were a team of student ambassadors, currently or recently graduated students, who could share their experiences of what it's really like to be a student in London.

The young people stayed in halls of residence in the centre of London and enjoyed a variety of evening events including a trip on the London Eye, a West End show and a look behind the scenes of the Victoria and Albert Museum. The students also enjoyed a personal tour of the Fashion and Textiles Museum by Zandra Rhodes who dyed her hair pink for the occasion!

The week ended with an exhibition of everyone's work – the tutors were very impressed by the quality of the work the students had created.

Masterclasses

Masterclasses are ways of linking able pupils directly with experts in their field. This can be done by video conferencing but is more likely to happen in an art and design context by allowing pupils to work directly with the expert, for example via an artist residency, or by working closely with an art college or university to provide activities and workshops specifically designed for them at the HEI and run by tutors there, using their specialist equipment, etc. By their nature, masterclasses can rarely occur on a regular basis as all have cost implications but they should be planned into units of work whenever at all possible. Summer schools are a form of masterclass, similarly teachers can organise their own one-day events in consultation with local universities, addressing a particular area of the curriculum that requires more depth and breadth than the school art department can accommodate – for example, extending the print-making process from classroom practice and offering a more able Year 10 or 11 GCSE student (or AS/A level if they are being entered early) or group of students the chance to work on a large print with a print bed and facilities for etching or large-scale screen printing with specialist tuition.

If your art department is running an artist residency, it is a good idea to hold after-school sessions which offer the chance for more able artists to work in smaller groups or on a one-to-one basis with the artist, gaining more insight into their methods and style of working. The added benefit of after-school sessions are that pupils from across key stages can attend so that they can work together because of their shared interest and ability, not their age. By offering some of the sessions to parents, grandparents and staff from neighbouring schools (cross-phase), the art department can widen its impact and further support its more able pupils. Alternatively, time can be allocated during the normal school day for more able pupils to be off timetable to work solely with the artist-in-residence on a set project that is continued with in future lessons.

Within your art department are teachers who are specialists in specific fields of art, craft and design. Why not ask them if they will run masterclasses in their chosen area for able pupils over the course of the academic year? You may have schools with specialist status in visual arts or media arts in your locality – part of their remit is to share their expertise and practice with other schools. Why not find out what they're offering and build it into teacher INSET time or more able pupils' collaborative working? Also, galleries such as Tate often have visiting artists speaking about their work in a current exhibition. Look out for any information on this and book in your more able pupils – they will probably ask the most interesting questions!

Appendices

Ofsted – Expectations of schools in relation to able pupils

Evaluation focus	Issue	Judgement/evidence
Effectiveness of school	Inclusion/equal opportunities	• High achievement is determined by 'the school's commitment to inclusion and the steps it takes to ensure that *every* pupil does as well as possible.' (p. 25) • At the parents' meeting, inspectors should find out if, in the view of parents, 'their children are progressing as well as they could; their children are happy in school, well taught and well cared for; the extent to which the school promotes equality of opportunity between different groups and includes *all* pupils and parents.' (p. 38)
Standards achieved by pupils	Achievement and underachievement	• Inspectors are asked to look at the achievement of different groups. (p. 44) • 'If they (pupils) are readily capable of work beyond that which they are doing, they are underachieving.' (p. 45) • A school should know 'how well gifted and talented pupils do and, where appropriate, how well pupils do in the school's specialist subjects . . . Inspectors should judge how well the school uses information to identify and deal with underachievement, challenge the most capable and raise standards for all pupils.' (p. 48)
	Early entry	• Inspectors should be aware of special circumstances, such as 'a school policy on early entry for GCSE for some pupils.' • 'Where pupils are entered early for GCSE examinations, inspectors should take account of the results in reaching a judgement about the performance of the year group as a whole and consider what early entry has allowed the pupils to achieve subsequently.' (p. 47)
	Discussion with pupils	• Inspectors should 'talk to pupils of different ages and levels of attainment (including) . . . the high achievers.' (p. 54)
	Assessment	• Assessment might guide planning through 'review of pupils' progress, including whether targets have been met at the end of a unit of work to inform teaching and target-setting for the whole class, groups and individuals.' (p. 88) • Inspectors should observe 'how targets for individual pupils of all abilities are agreed . . .' (p. 88) • Inspectors should take samples of students' work to see 'how assessment contributes to planning work for gifted and talented pupils . . . and how the outcomes are considered in reviews.' (p. 88)

Evaluation focus	Issue	Judgement/evidence
Quality of education	Teachers' command of subject	• 'Pupils should be learning from experts.' • 'Teachers' knowledge is demonstrated in the way they . . . cater for the more able in a subject.' (p. 77)
	Appropriate challenge	• 'Effective teaching extends pupils intellectually, creatively and physically. Inspectors should judge whether teachers are determined to get the best out of the pupils and if they are being challenged enough.' (p. 78) • Inspectors are advised to 'observe what is done to challenge the most able pupils in the class, including those who may be identified by the school as gifted and talented. Watch for those pupils who are clearly not being challenged enough. What is the effect of lack of challenge on them? Where no obvious special provision is being made, find out why.' (p. 81)
	Learning methods and resources	• Judge the approaches used for pupils of high ability' (p. 79) • Inspectors should assess whether 'teachers involve all pupils in lessons, giving the diffident and the slower learners a chance to contribute and time to answer questions, and yet challenging the most able.' (p. 75)
	Homework	• 'How well is homework tailored to individual needs and capabilities?' (p. 81)
	Equality of access (to the curriculum)	• 'Does it take account of their cultural background and religious beliefs, diverse ethnic backgrounds, special educational needs and particular gifts or talents?' (p. 100)
	Pupil care	• Evidence of the care of pupils will include provision for those who are gifted and talented. (p. 109)
Management	Inclusion	• Does the school provide successfully for pupils who . . . are gifted and talented?' (p. 144)
Schools causing concern	Underachieving schools	• 'Triggers that might suggest a school is underachieving include: . . . lack of challenge and slow progress for particular groups of pupils (for example the most able), in certain classes, a particular stage or in several subjects.' (p. 164)
Initiatives for raising achievement	Excellence in Cities	• 'Gifted and Talented pupils should be identified in EiC schools . . . The school should have a policy and teaching programme for these pupils. Inspectors should evaluate the effectiveness of the school's strategy in motivating gifted and talented pupils and ensuring that they achieve as well as they can both in lessons and extracurricular activities.' (p. 30)

The page numbers refer to the Ofsted *Handbook for Inspecting Secondary Schools* (2003).

From *Meeting the Needs of Your Most Able Pupils: Art*, David Fulton Publishers 2006

National quality standards in gifted and talented education

Generic Elements	Entry	Developing	Exemplary
	A – Effective teaching and learning strategies		
1. Identification	i. The school/college has learning conditions and systems to identify gifted and talented pupils in all year groups and an agreed definition and shared understanding of the meaning of 'gifted and talented' within its own, local and national contexts	i. Individual pupils are screened annually against clear criteria at school/college and subject/topic level	i. **Multiple criteria** and **sources of evidence** are used to identify gifts and talents, including through the use of a broad range of quantitative and qualitative data
	ii. An **accurate record** of the identified gifted and talented population is kept and updated.	ii. The record is used to identify under-achievement and **exceptional achievement** (both within and outside the population) and to track/review pupil **progress**	ii. The record is supported by a comprehensive monitoring, progress planning and reporting system which all staff regularly share and contribute to
	iii. The identified gifted and talented population broadly reflects the school/college's **social and economic composition**, gender and ethnicity	iii. **Identification** systems address issues of **multiple exceptionality** (pupils with specific gifts/talents and special educational needs)	iii. **Identification** processes are regularly reviewed and refreshed in the light of pupil performance and value-added data. The gifted and talented population is fully repre-sentative of the school/college's population
Evidence			
Next steps			
2. Effective provision in the classroom	i. The school/college addresses the different needs of the gifted and talented population by providing a stimulating learning environment and by extending the teaching repertoire	i. Teaching and learning strategies are diverse and flexible, meeting the needs of distinct pupil groups within the gifted and talented population (e.g. able underachievers, exceptionally able)	i. The school/college has established a range of methods to find out what works best in the classroom, and shares this within the school/college and with other schools and colleges
	ii. Teaching and learning is differentiated and delivered through both individual and group activities	ii. A range of challenging learning and teaching strategies is evident in lesson planning and delivery. **Independent learning** skills are developed.	ii. Teaching and learning are suitably challenging and varied, incorporating the **breadth, depth** and **pace** required to progress high achievement. Pupils routinely work independently and self-reliantly

	Entry	Developing	Exemplary
	iii. Opportunities exist to extend learning through **new technologies**	iii. The use of **new technologies** across the curriculum is focused on **personalised learning** needs	iii. The innovative use of **new technologies** raises the achievement and motivation of gifted and talented pupils
Evidence			
Next steps			
3. Standards	i. Levels of **attainment** and **achievement** for gifted and talented pupils are comparatively high in relation to the rest of the school/college population and are in line with those of similar pupils in similar schools/colleges	i. Levels of **attainment** and **achievement** for gifted and talented pupils are broadly consistent across the gifted and talented population and above those of similar pupils in similar schools/colleges	i. Levels of **attainment** and **achievement** for gifted and talented pupils indicate sustainability over time and are well above those of similar pupils in similar schools/colleges
	ii. Self-evaluation indicates that gifted and talented provision is satisfactory	ii. Self-evaluation indicates that gifted and talented provision is good	ii. Self-evaluation indicates that gifted and talented provision is very good or excellent
	iii. Schools/colleges gifted and talented education programmes are explicitly linked to the achievement of SMART outcomes and these highlight improvements in pupils' attainment and achievement		
Evidence			
Next steps			

B – Enabling curriculum entitlement and choice

	Entry	Developing	Exemplary
4. Enabling curriculum entitlement and choice	i. Curriculum organisation is flexible, with opportunities for enrichment and increasing subject/topic choice. Pupils are provided with support and guidance in making choices	i. The curriculum offers opportunities and guidance to pupils which enable them to work beyond their age and/or phase, and across subjects or topics, according to their aptitudes and interests	i. The curriculum offers **personalised learning pathways** for pupils which maximise individual **potential**, retain flexibility of future choices, extend well beyond test/examination requirements and result in sustained impact on pupil **attainment and achievement**
Evidence			
Next steps			

Definitions for words and phrases in bold are provided in the glossary in the Quality Standards *User Guide*, available at www2.teachernet.gov.uk/gat.

Generic Elements	Entry	Developing	Exemplary
		C – Assessment for learning	
5. Assessment for learning	i. Processes of data analysis and pupil assessment are employed throughout the school/college to plan learning for gifted and talented pupils	i. Routine progress reviews, using both qualitative and quantitative data, make effective use of prior, predictive and value-added **attainment** data to plan for progression in pupils' learning	i. **Assessment data** are used by teachers and across the school/college//college to ensure challenge and sustained progression in individual pupils' learning
	ii. Dialogue with pupils provides focused feedback which is used to plan future learning	ii. Systematic oral and written feedback helps pupils to set challenging curricular targets	ii. Formative assessment and individual target-setting combine to maximise and celebrate pupils' achievements
	iii. Self and peer assessment, based on clear understanding of criteria, are used to increase pupils' responsibility for learning	iii. Pupils reflect on their own skill development and are involved in the design of their own targets and tasks	iii. Classroom practice regularly requires pupils to reflect on their own **progress** against targets, and engage in the direction of their own learning
Evidence			
Next steps			
6. Transfer and transition	i. Shared processes, using agreed criteria, are in place to ensure the productive transfer of information from one setting to another (i.e. from class to class, year to year and school/college to school/college)	i. Transfer information concerning gifted and talented pupils, including parental input, informs targets for pupils to ensure **progress** in learning. Particular attention is given to including new admissions	i. Transfer data concerning gifted and talented pupils are used to inform planning of teaching and learning at subject/aspect/topic and individual pupil level, and to ensure progression according to ability rather than age or phase
Evidence			
Next steps			
		D – School/College organisation	
7. Leadership	i. A named member of the governing body, senior management team and the lead professional responsible for gifted and talented education have clearly directed responsibilities for motivating and driving gifted and talented provision. The head teacher actively champions gifted and talented provision	i. **Responsibility** for gifted and talented provision is **distributed**, and evaluation of its impact shared, at all levels in the school/college. Staff subscribe to policy at all levels. Governors play a significant supportive and evaluative role	i. Organisational structures, communication channels and the deployment of staff (e.g. workforce remodelling) are flexible and creative in supporting the delivery of **personalised learning**. Governors take a lead in celebrating achievements of gifted and talented pupils
Evidence			
Next steps			

	Entry	Developing	Exemplary
8. Policy	i. The gifted and talented policy is integral to the school/college's inclusion agenda and approach to personalised learning, feeds into and from the single school/college improvement plan and is consistent with other policies	i. The policy directs and reflects best practice in the school/college, is regularly reviewed and is clearly linked to other policy documentation	i. The policy includes input from the whole school/college community and is regularly refreshed in the light of innovative national and international practice
Evidence			
Next steps			
9. School/College ethos and pastoral care	i. The school/college sets high expectations, recognises achievement and celebrates the successes of all its pupils	i. The school/college fosters an environment which promotes positive behaviour for learning. Pupils are listened to and their views taken into account.	i. An ethos of ambition and achievement is agreed and shared by the whole school/college community. Success across a wide range of abilities is celebrated
	ii. The school/college identifies and addresses the particular social and emotional needs of gifted and talented pupils in consultation with pupils, parents and carers	ii. Strategies exist to counteract bullying and any adverse effects of social and curriculum pressures. Specific support for able underachievers and pupils from different cultures and social backgrounds is available and accessible	ii. The school/college places equal emphasis on high achievement and emotional well-being, underpinned by programmes of support personalised to the needs of gifted and talented pupils. There are opportunities for pupils to use their gifts to benefit other pupils and the wider community
Evidence			
Next steps			
10. Staff development	i. Staff have received professional development in meeting the needs of gifted and talented pupils	i. The induction programme for new staff addresses gifted and talented issues, both at whole school/college and specific subject/aspect level	i. There is **ongoing audit of staff needs** and an appropriate range of professional development in gifted and talented education. Professional development is informed by research and collaboration within and beyond the school/college

Definitions for words and phrases in bold are provided in the glossary in the Quality Standards *User Guide*, available at www2.teachernet.gov.uk/gat.

© Crown copyright 2005

Generic Elements	Entry	Developing	Exemplary
	ii. The lead professional responsible for gifted and talented education has received appropriate professional development	ii. Subject/aspect and phase leaders have received specific professional development in meeting the needs of gifted and talented pupils	ii. Priorities for the development of gifted and talented provision are included within a professional development entitlement for all staff and are monitored through performance management processes
Evidence			
Next steps			
11. Resources	i. Provision for gifted and talented pupils is supported by appropriate budgets and resources	i. Allocated resources include school/college based and nationally available resources, and these have a significant and measurable impact on the progress that pupils make and their attitudes to learning	i. Resources are used to stimulate innovative and experimental practice, which is shared throughout the school/college and which are regularly reviewed for impact and best value
Evidence			
Next steps			
12. Monitoring and evaluation	i. **Subject and phase audits** focus on the quality of teaching and learning for gifted and talented pupils. Whole school/college targets are set using prior **attainment** data	i. Performance against targets (including at pupil level) is regularly reviewed. Targets include qualitative pastoral and curriculum outcomes as well as numerical data	i. Performance against targets is rigorously evaluated against clear criteria. Qualitative and quantitative outcomes inform whole school/college self-evaluation processes
	ii. Elements of provision are planned against clear objectives within effective whole-school self-evaluation processes	ii. All elements, including non-academic aspects of gifted and talented provision are planned to clear objectives and are subjected to detailed evaluation	ii. The school/college examines and challenges its own provision to inform development of further experimental and innovative practice in collaboration with other schools/colleges
Evidence			
Next steps			

E – Strong partnerships beyond the school

13. Engaging with the community, families and beyond	i. Parents/carers are aware of the school's/college's policy on gifted and talented provision, contribute to its **identification** processes and are kept informed of developments in gifted and talented provision, including through the School Profile	i. Progression of gifted and talented pupils is enhanced by home-school/college partnerships. There are strategies to engage and support hard-to-reach parents/carers	i. Parents/carers are actively engaged in extending provision. Support for gifted and talented provision is integrated with other children's services (e.g. Sure Start, EAL, traveller, refugee, **LAC** Services)	
	ii. The school/college shares good practice and has some collaborative provision with other schools, colleges and the wider community	ii. A coherent strategy for networking with other schools, colleges and local community organisations extends and enriches provision	ii. There is strong emphasis on collaborative and innovative working with other schools/colleges which impacts on quality of provision locally, regionally and nationally	
Evidence				
Next steps				
14. Learning beyond the classroom	i. There are opportunities for pupils to learn beyond the school/college day and site (extended hours and out-of-school activities)	i. A coherent programme of enrichment and extension activities (through extended hours and out-of-school activities) complements teaching and learning and helps identify pupils' latent gifts and talents	i. Innovative models of learning beyond the classroom are developed in collaboration with local and national schools/colleges to further enhance teaching and learning	
	ii. Pupils participate in dedicated gifted and talented activities (e.g. summer schools) and their participation is recorded	ii. Local and national provision helps meet individual pupils' learning needs e.g. NAGTY membership, accessing outreach, local enrichment programmes	ii. Coherent strategies are used to direct and develop individual expert performance via external agencies e.g. HE/FE links, on-line support, and local/regional/national programmes	
Evidence				
Next steps				

Definitions for words and phrases in bold are provided in the glossary in the Quality Standards *User Guide*, available at www2.teachernet.gov.uk/gat.

© Crown copyright 2005

ART DEPARTMENT
Higher Ability Group (HAG) departmental procedure

Identification

Year 7 level predictions

Art teachers will make predictions for Key Stage 3 grades based on work produced each term during Year 7. Predictions will be triangulated at the end of the year to confirm overall predictions. This information will form the basis of identification of the Higher Ability Group (HAG).

Criteria for inclusion

Pupils identified will display a high level of interest and skill in art. They will regularly complete homework and maintain a high standard in both class work and homework.

End-of-year departmental verification meeting

The purpose of the meeting is threefold:

1. triangulation of Year 7 level predictions

2. triangulation of data based on Year 8 performance

3. confirmation of attainment of Year 7/8 at Year 9

Continuity

Year 8 HAG pupils will be invited to continue membership into Year 9 provided that their performance merits inclusion.

Non-membership for the group in Year 8 does not preclude membership at Year 9. Art staff will monitor such development during the course of the year. Level 7 is attainable by any pupil irrespective of HAG membership.

Level 8

Pupils who consistently perform at an exceptionally high standard may be considered able to reach Level 8. Such pupils should be identified at the Christmas termly assessment and informed what is required at Level 8.

Communication

September induction meeting

Meetings will be called each September at which pupils will be given the information they need to embark on work towards Level 7.

NC Documentation KS3

HAG pupils will be given a sheet explaining how membership of the HAG works and what is required for attainment of Level 7 and Level 8 as appropriate.

Regular discussion of work during lesson time

Teachers regularly discuss work with all pupils. It is important that teachers make time to discuss the extra requirements at Level 7 with relevant pupils.

Regular marking of sketch books

Teacher comments in sketch books will provide a regular means of communication with pupils.

Termly formal assessment of work

All HAG pupils will submit their sketch books at the end of each term for assessment by all art teachers. They will receive formal confirmation regarding the level at which they are working.

PASS reporting system

The PASS reporting system will provide a further formal means of communication.

Class work provision

SoW to include extension work for class work

SoW will provide extension work for pupils who have completed normal class work before other pupils or for those who can miss a stage due to their high ability. Members of HAG will not necessarily be expected to complete the extension work.

Regular feedback and discussion of work with pupils during lesson

Teachers will regularly make a point of discussing with HAG pupils progressing towards their targets.

Homework extension work

Homework task sheets

These will include compulsory homework tasks for all pupils as well as optional extension work. All pupils may complete extension work if they wish. HAG pupils will be given differentiated homework according to their ability.

Marking

Because of the project-based nature of extension work, teachers may, if they wish, just write comments on HAG homework (i.e. not give a 'mark'). Pupils need to be informed as to the marking system and will need regular feedback regarding their progress.

Feedback

Pupils should hand in their homework regularly to their teachers so as to receive feedback and guidance. It is inappropriate to hand work in just at the end of term.

Enrichment activities

Lunchtime art club

Two days per week, lunchtime sessions will be reserved for KS3 pupils. This will provide an excellent opportunity for HAG pupils to complete extension work and discuss their progress.

Twilight sessions

Twilight sessions also provide an excellent opportunity for HAG pupils to complete extension or different work and discuss their progress.

G&T coordinator award

The G&T coordinator award provides an additional incentive for pupils to work to the best of their ability.

G&T fund materials support

Provision to all HAG members of a good quality sketchbook financed by the G&T fund also provides an additional incentive for pupils to work to the best of their ability.

Tracking

Assessment

Class work will be assessed as normal. HAG pupils will be expected to maintain high marks throughout the year.

Homework will be assessed regularly and pupils will receive regular feedback.

Monitoring

Records of termly formal assessment to be kept. Pupils struggling to maintain standards will be informed as to what is required of them.

Visual record

Photographic image bank

At the end of each year, a digital photographic record will be kept of selected sets of work by HAG pupils.

HEADS OF DEPARTMENT
Internal gifted and talented audit

School: . . . .   Subject: . . . .

Head of department: . . . .   No. in department: . . . .

1	Are all staff in your department conversant with the strategies employed in the teaching and learning provision for G&T students? E.g. Creative/critical thinking, HOTS (higher order thinking skills, from Bloom's taxonomy), VAK (visual/auditory/kinaesthetic thinking skills), multiple intelligences	Yes ☐ If yes please state INSET attended, school, LEA or other	No ☐ If no please state further support needed
2	Is the whole-school G&T policy effective in influencing classroom provision?	Yes ☐	No ☐ If no, please state reasons:
3	Have you developed a subject-specific policy? Have you revised units of work to encompass this? (Please attach one example of a revised unit of work that highlights discrete provision/extension tasks for G&T pupils)	Yes ☐ Yes ☐ In the process ☐	No ☐ No ☐
4	Are the G&T pupils clearly identified in subject registers?	Yes ☐ School cohort Yes ☐ Shadow cohort	No ☐
5	How do you monitor the progress of your G&T pupils?		
	Does a portfolio of outstanding work exist in your department?	Yes ☐	No ☐
6	Are pupils accelerated or fast-tracked in your subject? If so, give examples	Yes ☐	No ☐

7	What additional opportunities does your department offer for G&T pupils?				
8	Has your department benefited from the school's G&T budget? Please give an example of how it has impacted on teaching and learning in the classroom	Yes	☐	No	☐
9	Is G&T provision discussed at departmental/faculty meetings?	Yes	☐	No	☐
10	In what ways does your department share practice/work with other departments/schools, e.g. via cluster activities/summer schools, etc. Have students taken part in LEA G&T masterclasses/workshops?	Yes	☐	No	☐
11	How many G&T students in your subject area have participated in post-16 masterclasses? Which one?				
12	How many students are entered for an Advanced Extension Award in your subject this academic year?				
13	What are the key issues in the education of G&T in your subject area?				

From *Meeting the Needs of Your Most Able Pupils: Art*, David Fulton Publishers 2006

ANYTOWN SCHOOL
Able pupils departmental action plan

Action	Person(s) responsible for action	Timescale	Resources/ funding	Success criteria	Person(s) responsible for monitoring and evaluation	How activity will be monitored

From *Meeting the Needs of Your Most Able Pupils: Art*, David Fulton Publishers 2006

Adaptable art, craft and design Key Stage 3/4 unit of work IDENTITY

About this unit

In this unit, pupils explore identity. They will explore their faces and/or hands as a starting point with discussions and annotated sketches as to why they link with their own identities, e.g. eye colour, winking eye, frowning eyes, clenched fist, feelings, character, etc. They will use a range of media to experiment with in this observational work – varying grades of pencil, coloured pencil, acrylic paint and watercolour. They will research contemporary artists' work and will explore identity through digital photography, role play, three-dimensional mask-making techniques, collage and, if time, transfer to textiles and fabric printing. Most pupils will consider their work in light of the quote *'identity lies in appearance, not in reality'* (information sheet on Sherman). *More able pupils will experience 'cognitive conflict' within Sherman's images and the above quote. They will modify and adapt their work in light of this research and consider presenting a 'false' image of themselves. They will have the opportunity to discovers aspects of the theory of Jean Baudrillard, the French Postmodern theorist and to incorporate similar thinking into their individual responses.

What the unit covers

ART CRAFT DESIGN	2D 3D	INDIVIDUAL WORK COLLABORATIVE WORK
LINE TONE COLOUR PATTERN TEXTURE	SHAPE FORM	SPACE
Painting Collage Print-making	Digital Media	Sculpture Textiles

Aims and objectives of this unit

At the end of this unit . . .

Most pupils will:
Analyse and comment on ideas surrounding identity or self-image and approaches to representing an image of self through shape, form and space; compare the approach of CINDY SHERMAN and their own work; record and explore ideas through role play and digital photography, developing and extending their skills; combining and manipulating collage and three-dimensional techniques to make a mask, exploring colour, pattern, form and shape; reflect on, adapt and refine their work to realise their own ideas and intentions.

Some pupils will not have made so much progress and will:
Comment on similarities and differences between CINDY SHERMAN'S work and their own; represent themselves through observational drawing and digital photography; experiment with collage and mask-making techniques to move from two-dimensional to three-dimensional work; adapt and improve their work.

*(more able) Some pupils will have progressed further and will:
Critically assess CINDY SHERMAN'S and others' ideas, methods and approaches and analyse their codes and conventions (e.g. Edward Hopper, Sherrie Levine); experiment with and select ideas, methods and approaches to use in their own work and interpret shape, form and space in two- and three-dimensional representation (observational work, digital photography, mask-making); explain how their understanding of 'identity', Sherman's and other's work has influenced their practice, making links with Postmodernist theory.

A) Exploring and developing ideas

Objectives: to discuss and question critically a range of visual and other information

Activities:

- Each student is given a small mirror tile each to make observational drawings in their sketchbooks of their own eyes (one open, one closed, frowning, winking, etc). They use a variety of media such as pencil (B, 2B, 4B), coloured pencil, watercolour and acrylic. The work will vary in size and several studies may fit on a page. Pupils should annotate the feelings conveyed by these expressions. Home learning: a half-face self-portrait with tone and colour. Pupils to bring in a photograph of themselves for next lesson.

- The teacher discusses the home learning as a group and the group marks the work by considering use of the formal elements and skills. The teacher then introduces the cognitive conflict quote 'identity lies in appearance, not in reality'. More able pupils discuss what this might mean in relation to their observational drawings and paintings and the background to their photographs of themselves (eg. Time and date taken, do they like/dislike the image? Why?, etc). In their sketchbooks, pupils make written notes or sketches next to their photographs to say how they would like to be depicted if they could choose, how do they see themselves/would like to see themselves? Why? The teacher will need to give support and guidance to some other pupils by considering role models, etc.

- The teacher gives out photocopies of the photographs pupils brought in last lesson. These are worked on top of with colour in a variety of media in an attempt to alter the appearance and to change the 'feelings' conveyed by the expressions in the photos. These are stuck in sketchbooks and more able pupils may introduce collage using further copies of the photos. The teacher then introduces the work of CINDY SHERMAN and gives out information sheets. The teacher should concentrate on the 'Untitled Film Stills' series of photographs, focusing on '#15'. Pupils form groups and have copies of some of theses images per group. They discuss and make notes on what the images are trying to convey. The teacher then gives prompts and asks them to think particularly about the 'genre' of the 1950s and 60s and the roles of men and women in society (cross-curricular links with History, PSHE and Media Studies). Here, more able pupils may support those who might struggle with some aspects of this. Home learning: Pupils find out more information on this and make comparisons with modern life. More able pupils are given a copy of Edward Hopper's 'Morning Sun' 1952 and asked to find out about him, his style of working and compare and contrast this painting with Sherman's 'Untitled Film Still #15'. They should be given the 'Work in Focus' sheet also.

B) Investigating and making

Objectives: to record and analyse observations using digital photography and role-play and to explore ideas for different purposes.

Activities:

- The teacher provides some props such as hats, scarves, aprons, ties, briefcases, etc. for pupils to experiment with in order to create the character they wish to be in their photographs. This is done in small mixed ability groups. The teacher should give a strict time limit on this.

- An introduction should be given, if needed, in the use of a digital camera and then one issued to each group. Pupils should think about their 'pose' and take it in turns to photograph each other. Each child should keep a copy of the images of themselves on their own CD as part of their e-portfolio. The range of images may include close-ups and full-length pictures and may be kept to a minimum of three per pupil. A technician or classroom assistant could print these images in black and white and give copies to pupils before the end of the lesson if possible. Those pupils particularly finishing early may wish to download their images onto a PC within the department and manipulate them to distort, colour or use masking techniques, using Photoshop 6 or a later version, before printing out. Again, their images may also be put onto CD for their e-portfolio as keeping them on the system takes up too much memory. Equally this can be done at home or in after-school clubs if facilities are available. It should not be assumed that pupils have access to a PC at home.

- Teacher demonstration should highlight specific making techniques to pupils when thinking about designing a mask as the next step. These might include using ModRoc on faces although care should be taken when doing this to ensure that skin is not sensitive, to assess potential allergic reactions, ventilation and the ability to breathe freely, with supervision at all times;

alternatively, newspaper tubes or rolls can be used to construct the framework of a mask, with newspaper strips and watered-down PVA glue then used as papier-mâché. Both types of mask can be painted with acrylics or collaged with different types of paper. Pupils should be directed as to the method they should use according to the ability of the child as one technique may take much longer to reproduce than the other, depending upon the size. More able pupils can be given the choice as an open-ended task and they may have their own ideas upon construction and materials. The teacher may wish to offer them the opportunity to print their images on to fabric as well as/instead of making a mask. This can be achieved simply by using specific transfer paper for PC printers that is ironed onto fabric. Pupils may then wish to create something with the printed fabric that again links back to the theme of identity or a theme within that of a contemporary artist's work such as Annette Messager. With these techniques in mind, pupils should sketch their ideas for what their mask might look like in their sketchbooks and refine these during out-of-school hours or at the start of the next lesson with assistance from the teacher.

- Once the main mask has been created, pupils can then apply their designs, etc, using paint. The images of themselves should have been printed out and photocopied for use as collage on the mask. These may have been worked further by more able pupils using mixed media on top of the printout/copy. Extra materials may be added to enhance the mask, such as strips of fabric or paper.

C) Evaluating and developing work

Objectives: to adapt and refine their work and plan and develop this further, in the light of their own and others' evaluations.

Activities:

- The teacher may ask the pupils in groups to describe how their work was undertaken and what led to its realisation. They may be asked to analyse how effective their ideas, methods and approaches had been in their piece of work, but also by referring back to the artists studied. Pupils may then evaluate each others' work prompted by the teacher through questioning such as: Which piece of work has the most original approach? Whose work links most closely with Cindy Sherman's? Whose mask/textile has made effective use of Form? Shape? Texture? Colour? Collage? Digital images?

- More able pupils should be asked about how their work has extended from the theme of identity to consider aspects of other artists' work and how their work has then changed as a result (enrichment). Their sketchbooks should be annotated with these comments or recorded in other ways, such as the teacher recording what is said on a Dictaphone or mini-disc recorder – this can be done with pupils of all abilities. Notes should be taken on the use of specialist vocabulary used by the pupils and learned since the start of the project.

- The teacher could then identify with the pupils the parts of their research, ideas process or making that need to be adapted or ask them to decide how these could be reworked to make improvements. Pupils should then record this in their sketchbook so that they can refer to it in subsequent projects or tasks.

Teacher checklist for evaluating progress

'Evaluating the extent to which a scheme of work encourages progression in pupils' learning in art and design' (extract from DfES The Standards Site: Principles for constructing a scheme of work):

- What is known about what pupils have already achieved when they enter the Key Stage and how does this affect the pitch of the early units?

- Which ideas and skills in art and design depend on secure foundation of practical experience?

- How can units be sequenced so that earlier work lays the foundations for later work?

- Are there opportunities for revisiting and reinforcing the ideas pupils need to understand and which some will find difficult?

- When ideas are revisited and reinforced, is it in a different context or using different activities?

- **How are pupils who have some competence or expertise beyond the levels expected in particular years challenged?**

- How far do the school's scheme of work and units provide opportunities for pupils, as they move through Key Stage 3, to progress:

From: exploring ideas and collecting visual and other information for their work

To: exploring ideas for different purposes and audiences, selecting and using relevant visual and other information to help them develop their ideas

From: investigating visual and tactile qualities in materials and processes

To: investigating, combining and manipulating materials and processes, combining and organising visual and tactile qualities and matching these to ideas and intentions

From: commenting on similarities and differences between their own and others' work and adapting and improving their own work

To: comparing, commenting on and critically evaluating ideas, methods and approaches used in their own and others' work, relating these to the context in which the work was made, and adapting and refining their own work to realise their intentions.

Cindy Sherman background information sheet

Cindy Sherman is an American photographer. She was born in Glen Ridge, New Jersey in 1954. From an early age she was drawn to the television environment which started in the 1960s – the way this era of new technology and mass communications could invade our homes and capture the imagination of the viewer or listener so easily. (*Jean Baudrillard, the French Postmodern theorist – 'Death of the Real' – mass media codes and techniques of representation that comment on contemporary society*). Sherman was also fascinated by disguise and makeup and the way actors and actresses could present a false image of a real-life person. When she left school she studied Art at Buffalo State College (1972–6), concentrating on photography, which she still feels is the appropriate medium of expression in this media-dominated civilisation.

Her photographic images are at a basic level, portraits of herself in various situations that parody stereotypes of women. A vast array of characters and settings are drawn from sources of popular culture: old films, television soaps and magazines. Sherman rapidly rose to celebrity status in the international art world in the 1980s with her series of black and white 'Untitled Film Stills' in various group and solo exhibitions across America and Europe. Among the sixty-nine 'film stills' taken between 1977 and 1980 are portraits of Sherman in the role of such screen idols as Sophia Loren and Marilyn Monroe but also *B-movie stars, film noir victims and European New Wave cinema stars*. Sherman's work depicts many moods: quiet introspection, sensuality and elements of horror and decay in the series from 1988–9. Her images from the 1990s are mostly caricatures of people from art history, with Sherman appearing as a grotesque character in period costume. Her ironic approach to this work carries the message that *identity lies in appearance, not in reality*. Sherman is mocking and debasing television, advertising and magazines – all the conventions of popular culture, even as we know it today.

Sherman's works can be seen in the Tate Gallery, London and also the Corcoran Gallery, Washington DC, the Museum of Modern Art and the Metropolitan, Guggenheim and Brooklyn museums, New York.

(Words or phrases in italics may be aspects of this information that more able pupils could research and explore in more depth and breadth.)

Work in focus

More able pupils could read the Cindy Sherman article from 'Tate' magazine as a background to this information or pupils of all abilities could role play the interview in class. This is downloadable from: http://www.tate.org.uk/magazine/issue5/sherman.htm.

> Here the teacher could insert a picture of Sherman's *'Untitled Film Still#15'* 1978 (Guggenheim Museum) as the main work upon which this project may be based.

Cindy Sherman's 'Untitled Film Stills' (1977–80) are a trademark of Postmodernist art and this series of images depict her in melodramatic 'snapshots' as if from B-grade movies of the 1950s and 1960s. 'Untitled Film Still #15' depicts the tough girl with the heart of gold. She sits at a window contemplating her life. Her clothing and pose suggest she is streetwise and aware of her sexuality.

In pairs, ask each other the following questions:

- Where is she?
- Is she on her own?
- What is she thinking?
- How does Sherman make the character appear 'vulnerable'?
- What other symbolism does Sherman use in the photograph?

To make the work more 'artificial', Sherman often includes a visible camera cord, slightly eccentric props and unusual camera angles. She also uses herself as the model rather then a recognisable actress or modern day celebrity.

More able pupils could compare and contrast this photograph by Sherman with Edward Hopper's 'Morning Sun' 1952 (Guggenheim Museum).

As a class activity or homework, pupils of all abilities but at different levels, may wish to compare Sherman's work with that of other related artists such as Sherrie Levine, Barbara Kruger, Robert Longo and Richard Prince.

Resource material for CINDY SHERMAN, Identity, etc.

www.tate.org.uk/magazine/issue5/sherman.htm
www.artcyclopedia.com/artists/sherman_cindy.html
www.cindysherman.com
www.tate.org.uk
www.artchive.com
www.guggenheimcollection.org/site/artist_work_1g_146F_3.html
'Cindy Sherman – the complete untitled film stills' (MOMA 2003) by Cindy Sherman, ISBN 0870 705075
'Cindy Sherman: Retrospective' (Thames and Hudson) Essays by Amanda Cruz, *et al.*, ISBN 0500 27987X
Sherrie Levine at www.the-artists.org

Gifted and talented good practice lesson observation

School:	Teacher:
Year:	Date:
G&T coordinator:	Subject:
Grouping i.e. mixed ability: setted (top/middle); streamed: banding (top/middle) etc.	

Planning

SoW (Is the planning in place?)	
Is G&T provision specific and explicit?	
Does G&T provision within each module* of work regularly occur? (*half term)	
Are specific learning objectives identified?	
Are specific learning outcomes identified?	
Are thinking skills strategies used?	
Do the activities include HOTS/HOQ strategies? Are they implicit or explicit?	
What other strategy is used to challenge G&T pupils?	
Optional comment:	

Lesson visit comments. (Observations to be shared with the teacher if agreed prior to the lesson):

The lesson

Lesson context:		

Lesson structure:		

Differentiation by task		Pupil as group leader	
Differentiation by resource		Pupil as teacher/demonstrator	
Differentiation by pace		Pupil with more demanding role	
Differentiation by starting point		Pupil grouping extending the role of G&T	
Differentiation by support		Independent research	
Differentiation by homework		Independent presentation of findings	
Thinking skills		Formative assessment processes	
Accelerated learning cycle		Low stress	
HOTS strategy		High challenge	
HOQ strategies		Mind maps/concept maps/memory maps	
VAK		Brain-based learning strategies	

Starter:
Connection; lesson objectives; main skills to be used; rehearse previous learning; the big picture

Activities:
Key questions; key teaching points; notes for individual needs; relevant resources; reference to homework

Plenary:
Reflection; drawing together KSU for lesson examples; question pupils re learning; make links; celebrate success

Differentiated homework:
Greater challenge: open task; independent research; presentation requirement

References

Art and design

Askari, N. and Crill, R. (1997) *Colours of the Indus: Costume & Textiles of Pakistan.* London: Merrell Holberton and V&A Publishers.

Earle, K. and Curry, G. (2005) *Meeting SEN in the Curriculum: Art.* London: David Fulton Publishers.

Gilhooley, D. and Costin, S. (1997) *Unclasped: Contemporary British Jewellery.* London: Black Dog Publishing.

KD Kaur Singh, A & R. (1999) *Twin Perspectives: Paintings by Amrit and Rabindra KD Kaur Singh.* Liverpool: Twin Studio Publishing.

Lucie-Smith, E. (1995) *Artoday.* London: Phaidon Press.

Powell, J. (1998) *Postmodernism for Beginners.* New York: Writers and Readers Ltd.

Rosenthal, N., *et al.* (1997) *Sensation: Young British Artists from the Saatchi Collection.* London: Thames and Hudson.

Taylor, R. (1991) *Artists in Wigan Schools.* London: Calouste Gulbenkian Foundation.

More able/arts provision

Achter, J. A., Benbow, C. P. and Lubinski, D. (1997) 'Rethinking multipotentiality among the intellectually gifted: A critical review and recommendations'. *Gifted Pupil Quarterly,* 41, 5–15.

Bloom, B. (ed.) (1956) *Taxonomy of Educational Objectives.* New York, Longmans, Green & Co.

Bloom, B. S. (ed.) (1985) *Developing Talent in Young People.* New York: Ballantine Books.

Brown, G. and Wragg, E. (1993) *Questioning.* Oxford: Routledge Publishers.

Campbell, L. (1997) 'Variations on a theme – how teachers interpret MI theory'. *Educational Leadership,* 55 (1), 14–19.

Department for Education and Employment (1997) *Excellence in Schools.* London: DfEE.

Department for Education and Employment (1998) *Extending Opportunity: A National Framework for Study Support.* London: DfEE.

Department for Education and Employment (1998) *Health and Safety of Pupils on Educational Visits: A Good Practice Guide.* London: DfEE.

Department for Education and Skills (2001) *Health and Safety: Responsibilities and Powers.* 0803/2001. London: DfES.

Department for Education and Skills (2002) *Standards for LEAs in Overseeing Educational Visits. Supplement to Health and Safety of Pupils on Educational Visits: A Good Practice Guide.* 0564/2002. London: DfES.

Department for Education and Skills (2002) *Standards for Adventure. Supplement to Health and Safety of Pupils on Educational Visits: A Good Practice Guide.* 0565/2002. London: DfES.

Department for National Heritage (1996) *Setting the Scene: The Arts and Young People.* London: DNH.

Denton, C. and Postlethwaite, K. (1985) *Able Children: Identifying Them in the Classroom.* London: NfER Nelson Publishers.

Downing, D. and Watson, R. (2004) *School Art: What's in It? Exploring Visual Art in Secondary Schools.* London: NfER Nelson Publishers.

Evans, L. and Goodhew, G. (1997) *Activities for Staff in Primary and Secondary Schools.* Oxford: Framework Press.

Eyre, D. and Marjoram, T. (1990) *Enriching and Extending the National Curriculum.* London: Kegan Paul Publishers.

Eyre, D. (1997) *Able Children in Ordinary Schools.* London: David Fulton Publishers.

Fisher, R. (1990) *Teaching Children to Think.* Cheltenham: Stanley Thorne Publishers.

Fox, A. and Gardiner, M. F. (1997) *The Arts and Raising Achievement.* Conference paper: 24–25 February 1997. London: Department for National Heritage, Lancaster House.

Freeman, J. (1991) *Gifted Children Growing Up.* London: Cassell Publishers.

Gardner, H. (1993) *Frames of Mind: the Theory of Multiple Intelligences*, 10th annual edn. New York: Basic Books.

Gardner, H. (1999) *Intelligence Reframed: Multiple intelligences for the 21st Century.* New York: Basic Books.

Gardner, H. (2000) 'The giftedness matrix: a developmental perspective', in Friedman, R. C. and Shore, B. M. (eds), *Talents Unfolding: Cognition and Development.* Washington DC: American Psychological Association.

George, D. (1992) *The Challenge of the Able Child.* London: David Fulton Publishers.

Hamilton, D. *Picture Thoughts – Art across the Curriculum.* Maryland: Hamilton Associates.

Harries, S. (1998) *Investing in the Arts: How to Carry Out a School Arts Audit and Compile an Arts Statement.* London: RSA Publication.

HMI (1992) *The Education of Able Children in Maintained Schools.* London: HMSO.

Koshy, V. & Casey, R. (1997) *Effective Provision for Able and Exceptionally Able Children.* London: Hodder and Stoughton.

Langrehr, J. (2001) *Teaching Our Children to Think.* Indiana, USA: National Educational Service.

Nottinghamshire County Council – Education (2002) *Able Pupils: Providing For Able Pupils and Those with Exceptional Talent.* Nottingham: NCC Publication.

Ofsted (2003) *Handbook for Inspecting Secondary Schools.* London: Ofsted (see www.ofsted.gov.uk/publications/docs/hb2003/sechb03/hmi1360-01.html).

Ofsted (2003) *Inspection of Local Education Authorities; Ofsted/Audit Commission Inspection Guidance.* London: December 2003 v1a.

Renzulli, J. S. (1978) 'What Makes Giftedness? Re-examining a Definition'. *Phi Delta Kappan,* **60** (3), 180–184, 186.

Robinson, K. (1999) *All Our Futures: Creativity, Culture and Education.* London: DfEE Publications.

Robinson, K. (1990) *The Arts 5–16: A Curriculum Framework.* Edinburgh: Oliver & Boyd Publishers.

Smith, A. (1996) *Accelerated Learning in the Classroom.* Stafford: Network Educational Press

Teare, B. (1997) *Effective Provision for Able and Talented Children.* Stafford: Network Educational Press.

Further information

Gifted and talented

- G&T WISE: www.teachernet.gov.uk/gtwise
- National Curriculum: www.nc.uk.net
- DfES: www.standards.dfes.gov.uk/giftedandtalented

Accelerated learning

- www.alite.org.uk
- www.brookes.ac.uk/schools/education/rescon/cpdgifted/home.html
- QCA: www.qca.org.uk

Art and design

- NSEAD: www.nsead.org/home/index.aspx
- Arts Council England: www.artscouncil.org.uk
- Resources for all Key Stages: www2.teachernet.gov.uk/gat

Specialist schools

- www.specialistschools.org.uk
- Artsmark: www.artsmark.co.uk
- Arts learning consortium: www.networkingthearts.co.uk/alc/home.html

ICT in art

- G&T WISE: www.teachernet.gov.uk/gtwise
- DfES: www.standards.dfes.gov.uk/keystage3/downloads/ictac_ad018804.pdf
- National Grid for Learning: http://forum.ngfl.gov.uk/WebX13@@.efa35aa
- School website: www.e-gfl/activities/intranet/teacher/art/SJP
- Article: www.pcallow.freeserve.co.uk/jade20.pdf

Artists

- www.axisartists.org.uk/home.aspx
- www.dorriehalliday.com
- www.grahamrawle.com
- www.antonygormley.com
- www.sculpture.org.uk

Galleries, museums, sculpture parks

- Tate Gallery: www.tate.org.uk
- National Portrait Gallery: www.npg.org.uk
- National Gallery: www.nationalgallery.org.uk
- Yorkshire Sculpture Park: www.ysp.co.uk